YOU MAKE THE DIFFERENCE

THROUGH

SUCCESSFUL GROUPS & PROJECTS

Kay Kay

In collaboration with Tim Kay

You Make the Difference
www.youmakethedifference.net

Second Edition
First Edition published in 2012

Book designed and published by Tim Kay
University of Life

www.unioflife.net

You Make the Difference logo
© Tim Kay
All other illustrations and images © Microsoft Corporation

Author photo by Lina&Linda AB
Stockholm, Sweden

Copyright © 2013 Kay Kay
All rights reserved.
ISBN-10: 1482700646
ISBN-13: 978-1482700640

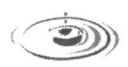

DEDICATION

This book is dedicated to all those people who are committed to making a positive difference in the world with their groups and through their projects.

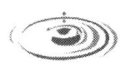

CONTENTS

	Acknowledgments	i
1	UNDERSTANDING GROUPS	1
2	CONSTRUCTIVE COMMUNICATION	24
3	LEADERSHIP	36
4	FORMING GROUPS	54
5	DEVELOPING THE GROUP CULTURE	60
6	STARTING PROJECTS	71
7	LEGAL AND MANAGEMENT STRUCTURES	88
8	ACQUIRING RESOURCES	102
9	PROJECT MEASUREMENT, EVALUATION, REFLECTION, REVIEW AND FEEDBCK	116
10	IT IS OVER WHEN IT IS OVER	130

ACKNOWLEDGMENTS

I'm grateful to all of those people in countless groups and projects from the UK to Siberia, Scandinavia to Central America, the United States to New Zealand from whose work in groups and projects I have learnt so much over the past half-century.

While initiating or supporting, consulting or coaching, volunteering or benefiting from so many groups and projects, it has been my privilege to meet some extraordinarily dedicated people making a huge difference in their local communities.

I am especially appreciative of my colleagues and friends in the Findhorn Community: www.findhorn.com whose group work is outstanding. To Sir John Whitmore, whose insights into the 3 stages of team development in his book, Coaching for Performance, has informed and inspired my work on the stages of group development, and to Lawrence Demarco of Social Enterprise Scotland: www.senscot.net for providing so many useful networking links and extremely informative articles and reports.

I believe that we all owe a debt of gratitude to those among us who see beyond their own immediate needs and are willing to offer their skills and commit time and effort to groups and projects that make a difference to the world around them.

1

UNDERSTANDING GROUPS

"Never doubt that a small group of thoughtful, committed citizens can change the world, indeed, it is the only thing that ever has."
Margaret Mead.

Perhaps this quote is even more relevant now than when Margaret said it so many years ago. Although there are relatively small groups of powerful people, not all of whom are democratically elected, who make decisions that affect billions of people, there are now billions of people gathering together in groups to make or influence decisions that make the difference to their own lives and to their communities.

> A small group of people working effectively together and supporting one another in their commitment to a project or a cause is a force of nature that takes some stopping. These groups are changing the world from the ground up!

While this book has been written with Voluntary and Community Groups and Projects in mind, the information it contains could be beneficial to many types of projects, organizations and almost any group.

What is success?

A group or project is usually considered to be successful when it succeeds in achieving the stated objectives. From experience I have learned that it is **how** a group or project achieves these objectives that is likely to make the most difference to those involved and beyond.

It seems to me that a successful group is one that includes in its objectives the development and wellbeing of its members and the intention to demonstrate the benefits of cooperation and mutual respect.

A living thing

A group is a living thing; made up of multiple personalities, each contributing different perspectives, motivations, experience and skills. It is the combination of all of these that forms the character and the culture of a group. How well a group recognizes and manages these differences, utilizes the strengths and handles the weaknesses can determine how successful that group will be.

Groups are ideal situations in which people can develop themselves through learning or improving skills, especially in personal communication and co-operative working. Such groups thrive when their members have, or learn to develop, attitudes of tolerance, openness, mutual support and respect. It is becoming obvious to many people that by modeling and demonstrating these skills and attitudes within their Voluntary and Community Groups they can have a positive influence upon society.

> What seems not to be so evident to many people is that it is mainly, perhaps only, when a society has these mutually beneficial skills and attitudes at its core that it is most likely to nurture its citizen's, protect the environment and be socially and financially sustainable.

Gathering together

It seems self-evident that the urge to gather together in groups is fundamental to being human. There are many beneficial reasons for being in groups, and, when there aren't any obvious reasons, we humans make some up. These are usually around work, sports, hobbies and innumerable areas of common interest.

Groups are usually formed for some common purpose:
a. To share an interest
b. To fulfill a common need.
c. To share a common task.
d. To achieve a common objective.
e. To develop and manage a project.

f. To pool resources.
g. To share ideas, information and experience.
h. To provide mutual support
i. To offer help to others.

Groups are often made up of people from different backgrounds, with a variety of skills, life experiences and different amounts of time and resources to offer.

Groups thrive if, right from the start, sufficient attention is paid to inclusivity, to creating group cohesion, and making conscious efforts to maintain it.

Some groups might not survive for very long without conscious attention being given to this. Even though groups might continue for some time, and although they may achieve many of their objectives, their interactions and activities could be full of friction and disharmony and offer little pleasure to their members, of which there might be a constant turnover.

Strategies

In any group, especially project groups it is important to develop strategies for achieving a variety of objectives. Different strategies will be required at different times.

At the start of any project or the formation of any group, it is wise to identify the purpose and objective aims, goals, desired outcomes and results and the appropriate ways of working together. When these are all clear the strategies for creating most direct path towards these usually becomes obvious.

Strategies will be needed for the following aspects:

1. **Achieving outcomes** In terms of achieving the desired outcomes, the strategies would be to identify the best ways for achieving the objectives, the means for acquiring any necessary resources — people, funding, equipment and services and pay attention to the plans for each step and who will do what, how, where and when.

2. **Gaining public recognition** If outside recognition or support is required then it will be important to have strategies for making those objectives public in the most appropriate ways.

3. **Sustainability** In creating a sustainable group culture the strategies would include establishing ethics and values; making group agreements around ethics, values, communication, behavior and

leadership; developing procedures for maintaining cooperation and dealing with conflict, managing meetings and making decisions.

4. **Maintaining effectiveness** To maintain the project's effectiveness and continued relevance the strategies would include methods for monitoring activities and measuring and evaluating results, procedures for feedback, ways of estimating continued relevance and exit strategies for when the group has achieved its' objectives.

5. **Working with volunteers** Whether you are in a group made up entirely of volunteers or an organization with some volunteer members, there will probably be a regular need for new members to replace those who leave or to help with an expansion of work. It will be wise to have strategies in place for identifying and recruiting the necessary and appropriate volunteers.

There can be some misconceptions and assumptions made by organizations where volunteering takes place. I have observed groups and organizations that believe there to be an unending supply of volunteers who can take the place of any who leave their service. This assumption can lead to volunteers being taken for granted or treated without due care and respect. In some cases this has resulted in those groups and organizations getting a bad reputation among volunteers.

This will be unfortunate in the coming years as the competition for volunteer help grows. It will be important for groups to have strategies in place for supporting, managing and keeping the volunteers that it already has.

Many of these strategies can be found in the book EMPOWERING VOLUNTEER MANAGEMENT in the YOU MAKE THE DIFFERENCE series, which is available from Amazon in paperback and e-book formats and accessible through our website: www.youmakethedifference.net/books

Creating Cohesion

To create cohesion and help a group to work well together, it would be beneficial for some of the members to have an understanding of how their group is likely to develop and function. This understanding will include some of these aspects:

A. Comprehension of the purpose and objectives of the group.
B. The importance of shared Ethics and Values.
C. Knowledge of the stages of group development.
D. Awareness of the group's culture.

A. Purpose and Objectives

For a group to fulfill its purpose and achieve its objectives it is important that everybody involved is clear what that purpose and those objectives are and to be in agreement with them. These might be obvious and be what people have been attracted to support. On the other hand, they may be vague or not clear to some people. It is surprising how often the purpose, goals, the aims, the intentions and objectives of groups are unclear to many of those involved in them. These objectives can sometimes be a vague sort of understanding among some people and even a wish, a dream or an ideal among others.

The fact that people have already come together around an issue might indicate what those objectives and intentions are likely to be. However, because nobody thinks quite like anybody else, there could be differing versions or a variety of thoughts about these. In their eagerness to show that they are doing something, groups might confuse *movement* with *action*.

Time spent in establishing the objectives and identifying ways in which they will be achieved can save huge amounts of wasted time and effort in the future.

Compatibility

It is important that the objectives of the individuals are compatible with stated aims of the group. Individuals can check this when considering joining a group or taking part in a project by asking those involved what the stated objectives are:

- Are these aims written down?
- Is there a mission statement?
- Are there minutes of meetings that record a clear statement of intent?

It might be useful to ask the existing members of the group what each of them believes the stated objectives are and how the group is doing in achieving them.

If the goals have never been stated clearly or if some in the group disagree about what they are, someone asking for clarity might help to improve awareness about this. If the objectives are uncertain or unclear it is up to individuals to decide whether this is a group to which they wish to commit time and energy.

> When those in an established group invite new people to join them, effort could be saved and misunderstandings avoided if the objectives of the group are clearly stated for the benefit of the prospective members. Those people could then be asked to support those objectives.

Mission statements

Having a mission statement or statement of purpose helps people to understand immediately what a group or an organization does. This statement needs to be clear, unambiguous and concise:

> "You Make the Difference is a virtual, global, Social Enterprise offering supportive information, books, e-books and free guides that can help people to make a positive difference to their lives and in society."

B. Values and Ethics

When a group is clear about its values and ethics it is likely to attract the people who have those same values and ethics.

When an individual is looking for a group or an organization to work with they will usually be looking for one that has the same values and ethics that they hold dear. This also often applies to funders and other supporters. More on this topic appears later in this book.

C. Group development

There are usually three main stages in the development of any group: The Inclusive Stage, the Assertive Stage, and finally the Co-operative Stage. Each of these stages can have significant impact on any group or project and upon the individuals within them. The identification of each stage would be useful to support the effectiveness of most groups and could be essential in supporting the sustainability of some.

These three stages are likely to clearly exist in long-term groups. In groups that are brought together for only a short time or a small project these stages might not be so easy to spot or there might not be enough time for them to have any significant impact.

With awareness, these stages can be easily identified. By paying attention to the behavior of members and the dynamics within the group it may become obvious which stage a group has reached in its development.

A closed group in a community setting is a rare thing. Most groups are open to people joining and leaving the group at any time. This means that whilst the group has a life of its own with identifiable stages of inclusion, assertion and cooperation, each individual joining the group at any of these stages of the group's development are likely to have an impact upon the process and go through their own personal stages of those steps.

Stage 1. Inclusion

This is when people are finding their place as part of a group. Anxiety, shyness and introversion are common and the need for acceptance and the fear of rejection can be strong. Group members might not be fully productive in this phase as their focus may be on the desire to fit in and be accepted.

On the face of it, for most of us, the wish to feel included in any group to which we belong might seem to be just a matter of preference. However, the need to feel included may be stronger than we first imagine.

The need to fit in and to be accepted by the groups to which we belong is deeply ingrained in human beings. It probably has its origins in humanity's distant past when societies were arranged along recognized tribal lines. The tribe provided protection, food, care and support. Individuals living outside of the tribal community might have been vulnerable to many dangers and being excluded from the tribe could have been life threatening.

These days, apart from a few remaining pockets of tribal existence around the planet, being in or out of a of group is rarely life-threatening, with the possible exception of extremist groups such as those involved in political violence, violent crime and gang warfare. Even so, it is a natural condition for we human beings to want to be accepted within our groups. The fear of being excluded or rejected can greatly influence behavior.

This need to belong can make people vulnerable to the behavior of others, especially to unkind behavior of insecure members of the group. This unkind behavior can include unwelcoming attitudes, bullying, gossiping and demeaning remarks. To avoid this, it would be wise for groups to be formed with some conscious awareness of the need to foster attitudes of welcome and inclusion and of processes that help to build trust and good relationships.

Fitting in

Some people seem to have the ability to fit comfortably into any group. They feel at ease wherever they are and with any person they are with. Those who do not may have different ways of attempting to fit into a group. They may be eager to seem friendly. They might show a willingness to do whatever is required of them. They can seem happy to conform to the values and ethics and the culture of the group or they may feel obliged to do so. They might appease people in leadership or dominant roles. They may slip into quiet acquiescence.

Some people spend much of their lives in this desire for inclusion and so devote a lot of time and energy to these 'fitting in' types of attitudes and behavior. Those whose life experience has left them feeling excluded or always on the outside, may need a lot of re-assurance before they feel fully accepted by others.

> For a few people there might not be sufficient assurance. These people might never leave the inclusion phase, no matter how long they are members of a group.

Individual self-management

As a member you can make the difference to your group by developing an attitude of welcoming newcomers and by being aware of and managing any of your own exclusion types of behavior - such as ignoring newcomers or excluding them from conversations, being disdainful or patronizing and making remarks intended to hurt or embarrass.

If you are normally shy or reticent to speak with people you do not know well you can use the opportunity of being in a group to make efforts to develop your social skills. You can be encouraged in this through the tolerance and understanding of other compassionate group members.

The leadership role in creating inclusion

The tone and the example that a leader sets in this inclusion stage is very important as this may quickly become the accepted norm for the group. The way in which all newcomers are welcomed into the group will affect how well they are accepted, how quickly they become integrated and how effective their contribution to the group will be.

Introductions

When the group is forming or when newcomers are joining, it is important that the introduction of potential group members is done with some conscious awareness. It would be helpful to have some process to assist people to connect easily with one another, which can then form the basis for the development of good working relationships.

There are useful introductory processes in our book: ENJOYABLE AND EFFECTIVE MEETINGS in the YOU MAKE THE DIFFERENCE series, which is available in paperback and e-book format from Amazon and is accessible through our website: www.youmakethedifference.net/books

If members are left to their own devices to connect with one another and to find their place in the group then group cohesion is likely to take an unnecessary length of time.

If new members are not carefully introduced into an existing group the group cohesion can be disrupted. Unless the group has a recognized inclusion process or the newcomer is experienced in groups, he or she might take time to become a useful member.

On the other hand, if new members are introduced with over enthusiastic reference to their talents and experience, some members of the existing group may feel that their place in the group is under some kind of threat. Their behavior towards newcomers might be influenced by feelings of insecurity.

> People feeling insecure may attempt to mask it with attitudes of indifference, condescension or aggression.

This can make it difficult for new people to feel accepted into the group and to easily offer their contribution.

Inclusive language

In most everyday communication it is usually beneficial to use 'I' statements. This gives the responsibility for the thoughts and feelings expressed in a statement to the person making it. This can help to prevent confrontation and any need for self-defense. However, in creating inclusion and maintaining cohesion in groups, it can be helpful to use a lot of inclusive language such as the words 'we' and 'us' and 'our' when referring to attitudes, behavior, decisions and actions within the group.

More information on other elements of Constructive Communications will be covered later.

The pecking order

This inclusive stage is traditionally where the pecking order in the group starts to be recognized. The polite term for this is the 'establishment of roles and functions', however, the words are often nicer than the actions. In the inclusion stage people who consider themselves to be leaders will usually make that evident. However, in less confident people or those who are manipulative - often the same thing - this jostling for position is usually covert.

Eventually, most members of the group reach the point where they feel included, accepted, at ease and comfortable within the group. This is when another stage emerges - that of individual assertion. Care needs to be taken at this time!

Stage 2. Assertion

This can be the time for extending personal boundaries and of establishing greater degrees of power. It is a phase in which people reveal their strengths and may attempt to use what they consider to be other people's weaknesses to gain some advantage. Covert manipulative behavior can become attempts at influence or dominance. This is the phase where assertion can easily turn into aggression.

These types of behavior may be tolerable in business organizations where people might be obliged to climb over each other for advancement. I believe there is no place for them in voluntary and community groups, organizations or associations.

> **There seems little point in working to improve the quality of life in society if we lose the quality of ourselves along the way.**

Time to assert

This is the time in a group's development when people feel confident enough within the group to share their wilder ideas, to put forward more radical suggestions, to be creative and to think outside the box.

It is also the time when people feel ready and able to challenge the ideas and suggestions of others, especially leaders, and to question the way things are done.

This is the time when timid mice can occasionally turn into roaring lions. When people who have always gone along with the crowd become stubborn, argumentative, difficult, and suddenly seem to want their own way. When quiet acquiescence - that may have evolved into silent resentment - suddenly is no longer silent; when the people who have previously had little to say make very sensible suggestions and come up with brilliant ideas.

These are rarely new characteristics that are emerging; they have usually been there all along. They have been held in check in the inclusion stage until people felt confident or safe enough to reveal them.

Double-edged

The assertion stage can be a double-edged sword! On one edge it can be a time of great creativity and energy as people get the bit between their teeth and move powerfully towards the group's objectives. This can be a competitive phase when a group may make up in productivity for what it loses in cohesion.

On the other edge, cracks may begin to appear within the fabric of the group. This can be a time of discord, when judgments and criticisms are thrown around; when decisions can be difficult to reach; when people might be accused of being awkward and when meetings can become unpleasant, lengthy and inconclusive.

This can be a time when people leave the group because they feel uncomfortable, frustrated or disappointed. This can result in the necessary workload falling on fewer and increasingly over-stretched individuals. This can be when progress just limps along or grinds to a halt. This can be a stage where groups fail.

Not the end

In the groups where there is little or no understanding of the three stages of group development it may seem at this stage that the group is falling apart at the seams. It may feel as though the harmony and the co-operation within the group have disappeared and have been replaced by aggression and dysfunction. This is rarely the case. The harmony and cooperation that seem to have disappeared might not have been there in any real depth in the first place. There was maybe only an artificial, pretend, on-the-surface, kind of harmony and co-operation that vanished when people felt themselves to be an integral part of the group and became confident enough to allow their real characteristics to show up.

> This is not the end. In terms of building cohesion this is the stage when the real work begins.

Individual self-management

Extreme assertion can quickly become aggression. Self-assertion over people who are in some way vulnerable is bullying. Being assertive does not mean belittling or demeaning people; nor does it mean being argumentative and it certainly does not mean being rude, verbally abusive or deliberately obstructive.

You can make the difference in your group by demonstrating how to avoid falling into these traps and assisting others to pay attention to the way that they assert themselves in any group situation.

Questions about ideas, queries about the methods of doing things or the offering of suggestions and differing opinions can be done respectfully and constructively.

> Constructive communication, direct speech, creative suggestions, positive thinking and inspiring presentations are appropriate and powerful ways of being assertive in a group.

Self-assertion about ideas and suggestions may take courage for some people at first. Group situations where everyone is working towards a common goal can be a very supportive environment in which to try out and develop some assertiveness. More confident members of the group could offer understanding, tolerance and compassion towards those who are attempting and perhaps struggling to improve these skills.

Permanent state of assertion

There are people who spend most of their time in assertive types of behavior. They seem rarely to have the need to feel included and accepted. They want and often expect to get their own way in all things and are likely to be persistent until they do. They may never become really cooperative; believing as they do that cooperation is something that others ought to offer to them.

Even though assertion might be essential if things are going to get done, permanently assertive people can cause havoc in groups. Words that are sometimes used to describe permanently assertive people are: bullies, power hungry, control freaks, dictators, demanding, awkward and insensitive. These people are often considered to be difficult to have in any group and concerns about having to deal with 'difficult' people are frequently cited as the reason why some people leave groups or do not join them in the first place.

When such people are the leaders of groups, other group members may be treated more as followers than peers. Although extremely assertive leaders can get things done, they often leave the wreckage of bruised egos in their wake. They might achieve the group's objectives only by railroading through ideas and by riding roughshod over other people's ideas and suggestions, protests and objections.

Through honest communication regarding concerns about such a person's attitudes, group members can help these people to manage their over-assertive tendencies and become more respectful in their behavior.

Using some of the methods described in the chapter on handling tricky situations in the book, ENJOYABLE & EFFECTIVE MEETINGS in this series could be beneficial. This is available in paperback and e-book formats from Amazon and is accessible through our website: www.youmakethedifference.net/books

Mo

I had a dear friend, Mo, who through a permanent state of assertiveness achieved a great deal in her life, although it also caused difficulties in her relationships and diminished her popularity within groups. With the help of her friends, she became less difficult to be with, without losing any of her effectiveness. As she gradually became more able to see herself as others saw her, she modified her behavior to some extent, which made it easier for more people to support her projects. She put a notice where she and others could see it that stated, 'I am not obnoxious; I am just tact-challenged!'

The leadership role in managing assertiveness

This important and valuable development phase can be tough on a leader. There may often be disagreements within the group and challenges to their leadership. Unfortunately, some leaders feel threatened by challenges, and so feel distressed or develop the need to assert their authority and to have control over the group.

I believe it is wise for a leader to allow some challenges to be made and upheld. An effective leader can encourage group members to satisfy their assertion needs appropriately, to take responsibilities for their behavior and to balance their own needs with those of the group. Effective leadership is a balancing act in these circumstances. If the leader displays openness and honesty and discloses some of his or her concerns and feelings or even some weakness, others may follow suit and good relating practices based upon integrity; self-disclosure and authenticity could be established.

Effective leaders will juggle the needs of individuals to assert themselves, the needs of the group as a whole, the ultimate group objectives and their own needs as leader as they support the group towards the cooperative stage.

Assertion may well be necessary to get things done, however, unless assertion is managed well the group may never move beyond this stage, which could have unfortunate results. For the cooperative stage to be reached, the dominating and controlling aspects of assertion need to be minimized or well managed.

Remember: Co-operation can be built upon a balance of the positive aspects of inclusion and well-managed assertion.

Stage 3. Cooperation

When the group feels inclusive enough for most members to express themselves with appropriate assertion then co-operation can quickly follow.

Individual self-management in co-operation

Co-operation in groups requires the following elements:
1. Mutual trust and regard between group members.
2. Understanding of and a respect for the skills and characteristics of all the group members.
3. A commitment from all involved to be supportive to one another.
4. Clear, honest and respectful communication among group members.

5. Willingness to compromise in order to reach the groups objectives.

The achievement of the group's objectives is more likely once co-operation is established because decisions can be reached with greater speed and ease; communications are likely to be more honest and straightforward; those in the group will understand their roles and carry them out with conviction and each person takes full responsibility for their behavior and their actions within the group.

The leadership role in co-operation

Harmony might exist for much of the time once co-operation is reached, although, the most productive groups can be highly co-operative and yet may retain a degree of dynamic tension. The most effective leaders preserve this with sensitivity. Apart from this, there is likely to be very little the leader may need to do to manage the group at this stage. The role can become more one of facilitation than management. This could include such things as:

- Having an overview of the group's activities in relationship to the objectives.
- Encouraging members of the group to take a leadership role in their area of interest or responsibility.
- Providing opportunities for discussions and the sharing of information.

Facilitation includes engaging in processes to improve communication and to support group decision-making. Some of the information in the book EFFORTLESS FACILITATION in this series could be helpful. This is available in paperback and e-book formats from Amazon and is accessible through our website: www.youmakethedifference.net/books

Individual contributions to group development

Obviously, individuals respond differently from one another in the various stages of their group's development. Some people have a real need to feel included before they are able to feel comfortable in a group situation. Some are rarely anything other than assertive. Yet others quickly reach and easily maintain a cooperative attitude. Most people will go through each stage to some degree in their group activities. It will be useful for the group members to be aware of these stages within themselves and when other members are demonstrating them.

Recognizing people's behavior is not to make them out to be wrong in any way. It is to realize that we are all human, that we each have our own ways of dealing with situations and making life work for us.

Groups are like families and intimate relationships in that they provide many opportunities for self-awareness and personal development through the interactions between those involved.

No matter how committed any of us are to a group or a project; no matter how strong our intentions might be to keep our less admirable behavior and characteristics from detrimentally affecting other people, at some stage, all of ourselves will show up. How well this is dealt with individually and collectively can determine how well a group will succeed.

It is obviously possible for groups to fulfill their purpose without anyone in them being aware of these three stages of group development. However, many groups without this information struggle along, often in strife or frustration and without much joy in their activities and interactions.

For a group to survive for any length of time, to effectively achieve its purpose and to provide an enjoyable and rewarding experience for its members, it is beneficial for at least one person in the group to have this knowledge and be strong enough to use it. This might be, although does not need to be, the overall leader of the group.

You can make the difference to your group by developing your self-awareness and to make conscious choices regarding your attitudes and behavior in each of these stages, and, by helping your group colleagues to do the same.

Those groups who reach the stage of working together co-operatively usually really enjoy the experience and get a great deal out of it. So much so that, when the original purpose for their coming together has been achieved, they may choose to find another reason for continuing to meet and to work together as a group.

D. Group Culture

It seems apparent that all groups have a culture. Regardless of whether it is a family group, a self-help group or project management group; whether it is small or large; whether its purpose is to do business, provide a service, run a country or just hang out together.

The culture of a group will include:
a. Values and ethics
b. Acceptable behavior
c. Communication
d. Loyalty
e. Ways for decision making

f. The feel good factor

The role of leadership in the group culture

The culture of any group is likely to be heavily influenced by the leader or the founder, at least in the early stages of a group's existence. The attitudes and behavior that become part of the accepted culture will probably be set by the leader and then permeate through the rest of the group.

The leader who wants to dominate, who treats people with disrespect, is overly demanding and looks for people to blame when things go wrong, is likely to influence a culture of uncertainty and mistrust. In this type of culture, members of the group often behave critically and judgmentally towards each other, are cautious about offering suggestions and are likely to put most of their energy into self-protection and self-preservation.

On the other hand, if the leader is respectful, inclusive and communicative, is open to suggestion and shares decision-making, then the group culture will probably be one of mutual respect, which fosters a high degree of willingness to participate among its members.

Even so, this top-down influence of group culture can be changed or moderated by the influence of other members.

Everyone will have an influence on the culture

Group cultures are living things that are forever changing and adapting to circumstances. In most groups, all members can be leaders in influencing the development of the culture of the group. A person who knows about interpersonal communications can lead the group towards a culture of good communication. Someone having an understanding of group dynamics and group development can contribute this understanding to the group's culture. Those with some particular skill or awareness can offer these:

- A person with skills in efficiency or cooperative decision-making can offer these to the group.
- Someone who knows how to motivate, encourage and appreciate people can have a significant influence on creating a can-do culture of mutual high regard and trust.
- A person who is naturally kind and supportive towards others can, by demonstration, encourage these to become part of a group's culture.

If you have any of these skills and experience then you can make the difference in your group by influencing the group's culture. Reading this book is likely to equip you to do this successfully.

Make a note

Make a note of the skills and experience you could bring to a group to make a positive difference.

Values and ethics

> It is surprising how few people go about their work and daily lives without consciously developing a set of personal values and ethics that influences and underpins their actions and behavior.

Many people have a religious belief that includes strong values and ethics, and yet, are these held consciously? How often are these demonstrated in all their thoughts, words and deeds?

With this lack of consciousness about personal values and ethics, it is perhaps not so surprising that many groups and organizations do not engage in processes to identify values and ethics to underpin their work! In my experience, the identification and establishment of Values and Ethics of a group or a project is an essential element to support commitment, effective working practices and ultimately sustainability. A process to establish these would be best done in frank and open discussion amongst all of the people involved.

> It is important that this process is not avoided or rushed. These values and ethics will underpin the actions of the group and support appropriate decision-making.

When they have been identified they can form the basis for the groups' agreements on practices and behavior. (More on this later.)

Communication

The way in which people in a group communicate with one another will say a lot about the culture of the group. When individuals join or are considering joining a group it might be wise for them to pay close attention to this. In my experience, the quality of communication within groups, organizations and projects has a significant effect upon their level of success. Because of this, the subject of communication is given a chapter later in this book.

E. Group Loyalty

Loyalty is a powerful element in the culture of any group. When achieved, loyalty bonds a group together and creates a sense of community and purpose that is extremely powerful and effective.

To develop loyalty the people within a group need to identify closely with the vision, purpose, values and ethics of the group and most importantly with each other. The closer they identify; the deeper the relationships can be; the stronger will be the harmony and bonding between them and the more effective and successful the group or project is likely to be.

Loyalty to each other is the most powerful antidote to 'blame cultures'. People are usually more willing to take responsibility and be accountable for their actions when they realize that making mistakes is a part of life that is best seen as learning opportunities. Learning from mistakes is far more likely to happen in a supportive environment when people help each other out when they most need it.

Taking the lead in loyalty

It does not have to be the overall leader who takes responsibility for creating a culture of loyalty in a group. Anyone within a group can take the lead in this.

> You can make the difference to your group by taking care how you communicate to and about others in the group. This will go a long way towards creating a loyalty culture.

This can be done through:
a. Using respectful language in conversations and in discussions.
b. Listen attentively and show that you value other people's opinions.
c. Avoiding gossiping about other group members and discourage it in your colleagues.
d. Speaking directly to people who have done or said things that have upset you rather than talking about them to others.
e. Avoiding judging people and if some criticism feels necessary make it constructive criticism.

For some people, loyalty to others in a group might be a new concept. In their places of employment, the groups in which they have previously been engaged or even within their families, people might have experienced a strong blame culture. Self-preservation and protection against this is likely to have resulted in a diminished sense of loyalty. Some people might have experienced loyalty as being something demanded of them and yet rarely given to them.

Remember: Although the work of building loyalty in some group cultures might take time, the benefits to the group, to the individual members and to the success of the project, could be considerable.

F. Decision-making

The way in which decisions are made is a significant factor in any group's culture.

In the making of major decisions within small groups it ought to be possible for all of the members involved to take part. In larger groups most major decisions will probably be taken at senior managerial level. However, decisions that will have an impact on the people within the organization or project ought to be made only after consultation or some level of engagement with everyone concerned. This can prevent people feeling resentful about having to implement decisions that have been taken without their involvement.

A resentful and disempowered workforce is bad enough when those people are paid employees; when they are volunteers it is a recipe for disaster.

People are much more likely to want to make any decision work if they have had a hand in making it. The people 'on the ground' as it were, are also more likely to be the ones with the most experience and information about the matter under discussion. To ignore this would seem to be a waste of a valuable resource.

To give people some autonomy and control over their involvement in any size of group, the small or day-to-day decisions would best be delegated to those people who have the responsibility for carrying them out. Having a chain of command for the making of little everyday decisions within a group is probably unnecessarily cumbersome and inefficient, might slow down progress and speed up disempowerment and resentment in the group.

There are several useful processes for decision making in the books: ENJOYABLE & EFFECTIVE MEETINGS and EFFORTLESS FACILITATION in this series, available from Amazon and accessible through: www.youmakethedifference.net/books

G. The feel good factor

For most people, feeling good in a group means having a positive experience of the factors we have already explored:
1. Feeling included and believing that they have some influence on what happens in the group.
2. Believing that they will be heard.
3. Believing that their views will be taken seriously.
4. Recognizing that they will participate in at least some of the decision-making.
5. Most people will also want to feel fulfilled.

Fulfillment

People join in groups and projects for all sorts of reasons and there are many ways in which people can feel fulfilled through their activities. Although each individual will have some specific aspects for their sense of fulfillment, there are some elements that are likely to be common to most:
a. The sense of achieving their purpose.
b. Being part of a successful team or project.
c. Pride in providing much needed help or support.
d. Belief that all their efforts have been worthwhile.
e. The recognition that they have made a difference.

Being valued and appreciated

A sense of fulfillment might include feeling valued and appreciated. Feeling valued in a group for most people means knowing that their contribution is respected and that their time, efforts and abilities are recognized. The less control people have over the decisions that affect their activities, the more appreciation they are likely to need in order to stay committed and enthusiastically involved.

There is a commonly held belief that service is its own reward and that people ought not to seek recognition or appreciation for offering their time, effort and skills to a group or project they believe in.

In my experience, any group or organization that operates under this illusion is likely to have some less than enthusiastic members and volunteers who may not stay around for very long.

Those who do stay may be doing so out of loyalty to colleagues or a deep commitment to a cause. Any advantage taken of such people will ultimately tarnish even the most laudable of causes.

By choice
People in business and professional working groups are often obliged to work together and to get on with one another as best they can. These groups may be able to maintain sufficient cohesion for a number of reasons: it is what is expected of them by their employers, they benefit financially, directly or indirectly, from the work of their colleagues and/or through mutual respect for the skills, professionalism and experience of one another.

It is important to remember that most people in Voluntary and Community Groups are there by choice. They are giving their time freely. They are offering their skills, expertise and experience because they want to make a contribution.

Small appreciations
A nod of acknowledgment or a word of thanks for things done well, completed on time or with good humor can let people know that their daily efforts are noticed and appreciated. This is not just something for leaders to do. Everyone in a group could contribute to an appreciative culture by behaving this way with one another. However, leaders can make a significant contribution by taking time in meetings and discussions to acknowledge and appreciate work done well.

Specific Appreciations
Appreciation and praise ought to be expressed as specifically as possible. Telling someone they are 'great' does not really tell them much about what is so great about them or what they are doing, and is often a hollow or meaningless form of praise. The point to appreciation is letting people know what has been noticed and valued about them and their work. Using expressions such as: 'Thank you for...' 'I appreciate the way you...' 'I can see how much you have...' 'This will help me to...' 'I am grateful to for you for finishing this so quickly. It gives me plenty of time to put this information into the report', will make this clear. Knowing what it is that they do well helps people to feel good about it and do more of it.

Immediate Appreciation
Praise and appreciation ought to be given as soon as possible after the event. A delay that separates the appreciation from the action might make it less meaningful. Saving the praising of someone until a group meeting is likely to have a less beneficial effect on that person if in the meantime he or she has been feeling unappreciated. Do both! Tell the person immediately

and then express the same appreciation in the later meeting.

Authentic Appreciation

I have noticed a tendency towards the use of over exaggeration in praise and appreciation such as Wow! Fantastic! Fabulous! Etc. Far from expressing a depth of appreciation, these words have lost much of their power from over use.

The same goes for the use of jargon. The fashion in the use of descriptive words probably changes more rapidly within cultures than in any other aspect of communication. Most age groups and common interest groups invent their own language of appreciation. Gear! Cool! Awesome! Wicked! These are examples of words that have been in and out of fashion in recent times. Using this kind of jargon is meaningless to anyone outside a particular culture. Doing so when the words are out of fashion, are not valued by the person you are praising or are not your usual way of speaking may make you appear ingenuous.

Direct Appreciation

Praise the person to their face. Telling other people how much you appreciate someone and hoping that information will reach that person will at best dilute that appreciation and make it less effective and at worst not reach the intended recipient. Do both! Tell the person and then tell others as well.

Simple, direct, authentic, immediate and specific appreciation of those around you will work wonders on so many levels.

When appreciation is at the core of a group's culture then the members of that group are likely to be supportive of one another and be willing to go the extra mile.

Separation and elitism

> In developing the culture of a group, care ought to be taken to avoid the traps of separation and elitism.

These can happen when those in a group feel that the culture of that group somehow makes them different from or better than other people, and separates them from those outside of the group.

I have noticed that when people have worked hard and consciously to develop a high quality culture within their group there is sometimes a tendency towards elitist thinking. There may be a reluctance to let some people into the group because 'they won't fit in' or 'they will not know how to do things our way.' There may even be a feeling, perhaps not directly expressed, that some people are 'not good enough' to be a member of the group. There might be some criticism of newcomers for doing things or for behaving in ways that the established group has moved beyond, 'That's not how we do things.'

Using this 'they are not like us' approach as an excuse for maintaining separateness from others is not an example of conscious development; it is more an example of entrenched and outdated human behavior. It is these attitudes that have separated people by race and religion, by color and creed, for millennia. It seems to me that there is no place for this type of thinking in a mutually sustainable and supportive society.

Establishing a group culture that has high values and ethics does not mean that the people in that group are better than others. I suspect that if this sort of sense of superiority exists in a group's culture, especially a community group, then there is still some work to be done on that group's values and ethics.

People who are attracted to a group that has consciously developed a culture of high values etc. are usually ready and willing to work within that group's agreements and guidelines. They may already have the same values and ethics as that group or are ready to embrace them. Perhaps their values and ethics are even higher than those of the group.

Some people might benefit from compassionate support as they learn and adopt the group's guidelines for communication and behavior. This type of attitude towards all members would most likely be built-in to a group that has consciously created a supportive culture.

Remember: A culture that helps a group to effectively and enjoyably achieve its aims while supporting the ongoing development of its members is a culture that could be an inspirational model in any society.

2

CONSTRUCTIVE COMMUNICATION

How we listen to and speak to one another communicates far more than just the words being conveyed in the conversation. It says a great deal about our character and in what kind of regard we hold the other person. Listening attentively and thinking before we speak not only enhances our personal and working relationships, it can be an indication of our maturity, especially our emotional maturity.

From my experience in studying, researching and working with interpersonal communications for several decades, it seems to me that a large part of what is being communicated, whether we are speaking or listening, is an intention to influence the feelings of the other person. This might be to influence how a person feels about us or to influence how that person feels about him or herself. This is the reason we will seem attentive when we are listening to some people and not with others. These are some of the reasons why we might say kind, caring and supportive things to some people and the opposite to others.

Our awareness of our intentions can vary from being completely unconsciously unaware of our ways of communicating; to making a conscious, deliberate choice in our way of speaking and listening to one another. Whichever it is, we will likely have an intention, conscious or unconscious, to influence the thoughts or feelings of everyone with whom we communicate.

For a group to work together cooperatively and harmoniously it would be wise to pay attention to the communication among the people in the group. Having Constructive Communication as an essential element in a group's culture could be very supportive to that group's effectiveness and sustainability.

Listening Constructively

People are listening constructively when they show that their intention is to listen and understand. There are a number of ways they can do this:
   a. By stopping what they are doing and giving their undivided attention to the person who is speaking.
   b. By allowing enough time to satisfactorily complete their conversation.
   c. By choosing suitable settings in which they can hear clearly.
   d. By encouraging people to fully express themselves.
   e. By listening with compassion and an open heart and mind: without interruption, judgment or criticism.
   f. By avoiding the temptation to give advice or fix people's difficulties before those people have had a chance to work things out for themselves.
   g. By clarifying anything they don't understand and check out that what they heard was what was actually said or meant.
   h. By making sure that people have said everything they need to say and have felt accurately heard and fully understood.

Speaking Constructively

This means speaking respectfully, clearly, directly, honestly, compassionately and supportively. People can do this by:
   a. Speaking respectfully to all people at all times.
   b. Saying what they mean and meaning what they say.
   c. Clearly stating their ideas, suggestions, opinions and conclusions.
   d. Honestly expressing how they feel about any situation.
   e. Avoiding leaving things out, covering up emotions, pretending all is well or denying what it is they want or need.
   f. Giving supportive feedback about what they observe.
   g. Speaking kindly and avoiding gossip.
   h. Being compassionate by avoiding making judgments and criticisms unless these are constructive and supportive.

If there is very little of this type of communication going on and people in a group speak unkindly, abrasively, disrespectfully or rudely to one another, there is poor communication within that group.

Poor communication happens when people listen and speak to each other in ways quite opposite to those listed above. From my research and experience I believe this type of communication to be much more than just poor; I believe it to be destructive.

> Destructive Communication is the opposite of Constructive Communication in every way, as are the results and consequences.

- Where Constructive Communication builds trust and mutual self-esteem – Destructive Communication harms both.
- Where Constructive Communication develops relationships and supports cooperation – Destructive Communication undermines both.
- Within a group context, Constructive Communication provides a foundation and a framework for effective, harmonious and enjoyable collaboration. Whereas, Destructive Communication often creates discord and rips at the heart of good will.

Individuals recognizing tendencies towards Destructive Communication within a group might reconsider being a member of that group. On the other hand, they might prefer to try to change the communication aspect of the group culture.

In bringing Constructive Communication into your group culture you may need to do so with compassion and respect. Compassion and respect for those to whom this might be a challenging concept. Compassion and respect for yourself as you endeavor to support this shift.

> You can make the difference to your group by eradicating damaging aspects from your communication and ensuring that your communication with other members of your group comes from the list of Constructive Communication stated earlier.

You could also introduce these principles to your group if they are unfamiliar to them.

It is crucial to not make anyone out to be wrong, bad or stupid if their ways of listening and speaking are sometimes the opposite of those listed, or if their style of communication could be described as poor or damaging.

To be unkindly critical of these people would itself be poor or damaging communication!

> It is important to remember that none of us know what we don't know.

Constructive Communication might not have been present to any great extent in some people's lives, and so, to those people, many elements of what I describe as Damaging Communication may seem quite normal and acceptable.

Mutually respectful communication might not be a keystone of the families or the culture in which some people live. Many people may not think about how they communicate. They might not associate their way of listening or speaking with the difficulties that they experience in their relationships.

Constructive Communication is rarely a priority subject in the school curriculum nor is it often an important subject in most professional training programs. It is my belief that if this were to change then many of our social problems might be irradiated in a couple of generations. Until that happens, we can all do the best we can to make a positive difference to the communications we are involved in.

Self-disclosure

The times when new people join a group can be used to consciously engage the group in some trust development. During some of the preliminary meetings, especially during the first one, time could be spent on people introducing themselves to one another in depth and in detail.

An aspect of building trust through communication is that of self-disclosure. This is when people talk openly about themselves, what's going on for them and how they are thinking and feeling. Unfortunately, this can be rare, even frowned upon or discouraged in some places.

Trust is commonly greater in groups where people know a lot about one another, either because of their shared history or because of information learned through their mutual self-disclosure.

To some people, self-disclosure might be okay within families or between close friends. However, it might feel uncomfortable or threatening for them within a group of relative strangers. This can create a Catch-22 situation where people don't feel safe enough to talk about themselves and what they're really thinking or feeling because there is not enough trust in the group. And yet, there isn't enough trust in the group because people are not being honest and open about their thoughts and feelings.

Obviously, when talking about yourself, your concerns, your ideas, your thoughts and your feelings within a group, or anywhere else for that matter, it is important to use 'I statements': 'I notice... I think... I feel... I wonder... I have concerns about... I am alarmed to hear... I feel it might be better if we... I would like... I need to... etc., are suggestions of effective ways to start a sentence of self-disclosure.

> You can make the difference in your project, group or organization by gradually and carefully becoming increasingly self-disclosing.

This can be a powerful tool for creating a change in attitude towards speaking openly. I have observed immense relief being experienced by people in groups who realize this gives them permission and opportunity to speak honestly.

Self-disclosure can also be introduced among group members by gently encouraging more of it in informal conversations, group discussions and in meetings.

If there is a strong culture of people being aloof with one another and keeping themselves to themselves within an organization then the concept of self-disclosure will need to be introduced with compassion and sensitivity. This could prove to be well worth the effort when openness and honest communication begins to underpin trust in your group.

Eradicating blame

In addition to self-disclosure, attention could be paid to eradicating blaming and shaming language within your group. When people develop the skill of talking about a situation without attempting to shift the blame away from themselves, or apportioning blame to others, the more opportunity there will be for trust to develop. The greater the likelihood for trust to grow is when things can be discussed openly, without any attempt to shame or embarrass the people involved.

Giving instructions

Constructive Communication is a firm foundation for the delivery of instructions or directions within the group.

> It is vital that the person delivering instructions knows exactly what these are intended to achieve.

Time is often wasted, or not fully utilized, because the people in charge of a task have not given sufficient thought to how best to give the instructions for it. This is inefficient and wasteful of a group's resources. In a volunteer situation, it also shows disrespect to those who gift their precious spare time for the benefit of the group.

For instructions to be fully effective they need to be delivered in a way that those receiving them can easily understand. They are most effective when given to the people with the appropriate skills and experience who have a sufficient amount of time available to carry them out.

To ensure that the instructions have been heard accurately a useful habit to develop within the culture of the group is that of requiring instructions to be repeated back by the person receiving them to the person delivering them. Whilst this may seem a little contrived, odd or even silly to some people, my experience is that this can save a great deal of time, effort and money.

Say something like: 'to make sure that I have included everything, please will you repeat back to me what you heard me say?'

You can also model this behavior by always repeating back any instructions that have been given to you: 'Let me check that I've got everything...' 'I want to make sure that I haven't missed anything...' 'I heard you say...'

If there is any doubt that some people within the organization might not be able to deliver instructions accurately, clearly and concisely, then it could be wise to create clear instruction sheets for some tasks. This could be helpful to newcomers and would be a sensible thing to do if there is a high turnover of volunteers.

Giving verbal feedback

Feedback given to other group members might be to appreciate them for what they are doing or to praise or complement them on work well done.

Feedback may of course also be to express concern about someone's actions or behavior, to tell them that they have made an error or to explain to them how something needs to be done differently. Even though it has only fairly recently become customary for people in groups to give direct feedback to people in leadership roles, this is fast becoming a part of many groups' culture.

The trouble is that some people have difficulty in expressing themselves or delivering feedback in an appropriate way. They might feel awkward, embarrassed or not want to risk upsetting people. So, they either, avoid saying anything and so give no feedback at all, in which case nobody learns and a situation is likely to worsen; or, they deliver the feedback harshly, as criticism or judgment, and in a manner that can be demoralizing and disempowering for the recipient.

Clear, honest, direct feedback does not need to be delivered in a critical or judgmental manner. It can easily be delivered with understanding, kindness and compassion. Using 'I' statement responses encourages people to take responsibility for their feedback.

Supporting improvement

We all make mistakes from time to time. We might not carry out instructions accurately. We don't always behave in the most appropriate manner. The whole point of feedback is to help one another to improve, to develop, to grow. We can all change our behavior and learn to do things differently or better. All we usually need is to be told in a way that we can hear and understand without feeling wrong, bad, stupid, hurt or rejected.

It is important to remember when delivering feedback that, even when you are making a great effort to do so supportively, you are likely to be challenging someone's actions, behavior or methods of communication. Hearing this can be uncomfortable for people, especially if they are not used to being challenged. Some people overreact or react very strongly to any form of criticism, real or imagined.

On some occasions, harsh responses might be directly aggressive and made for the benefit of the person delivering them. Often, someone's intention when delivering aggressive kinds of feedback is to vent their anger or to relieve their frustration. Or, it might be to seek revenge on that person or to make himself or herself feel better through embarrassing or humiliating that person. On the occasions when no direct response is made or a person is discounted or ignored; that is a passive form of aggression.

It seems to me that there is no need for any of this unkind feedback, which I suggest would fit under the heading of Destructive Communication. In my experience, this kind of feedback is rarely beneficial to anyone and often undermines the self-esteem of the person receiving the feedback; damages the relationship between the two people involved and can create problems for the group.

Remember: There is always a supportive way to deliver feedback constructively, even when people have made errors or their behavior, communication or actions have been inappropriate or have created problems.

Creating a feedback sandwich

Feedback that might be uncomfortable for someone to hear could best be delivered in a 'feedback sandwich'. That is achieved by saying something that might be uncomfortable for someone to hear in between two slices of appreciation, encouragement or praise.

Feedback that is constructive contains a clear statement of the situation, a description of how the person giving the feedback thinks and feels about it and a request or a suggestion for that kind of situation to be handled differently in the future. This is what I call a complete feedback message.

Complete Feedback Messages

> When offering this type of feedback we include these four elements: What we see; what we think; what we feel; and what we need, would wish or would prefer to happen next or in the future.

All relationships thrive on complete messages. People can't know the true reality of a situation unless we share all our experience of it. It means giving accurate feedback about what we observe and clearly stating our thoughts and conclusions. It means saying how we feel, what we need and making straightforward requests or suggestions if we see possibilities for improvement or change.

Leaving any of these out of a feedback message can create confusion and distrust for the following reasons:
1. People could be antagonized or turned off when they receive judgmental remarks.
2. They are likely to be defensive when they feel they are being criticized or interrogated.
3. They may be suspicious of conclusions arrived at that are not supported by observations.

> People who are defensive, angry, suspicious or turned off, are unlikely to clearly hear and accept the feedback they are given.

Creating Complete Feedback messages

The idea of a complete message is to deliver information to people about their actions, communication or behavior and your response to those in a holistic way to avoid misunderstandings and hurt. To say things in a way that people will be able to hear comfortably and understand what you are saying without becoming defensive or argumentative.

> Complete feedback is best kept simple, informative, honest, direct and spoken in a calm and respectful manner.

STEW
An easy way to remember the elements needed for a feedback message to be complete is to make a stew:
- **S** See: what you notice/observe.
- **T** Think: what you think about the situation.
- **E** Emotion: how you feel about it.
- **W** Want: what it is you wish, want or would like to happen next or in future similar situations.

With practice, you can learn to quickly put together a complete feedback message for every occasion with family, friends, in meetings, and in most situations in the workplace.

It may take a little time to retrain yourself to not react to things that upset you. However, if you can do this, and make the effort to create and deliver your feedback to people in a way that they can hear it and learn from it, your relationships could improve, and you are more likely to achieve the results you want.

Delivering Complete Feedback

Make your feedback direct
You know what you really want to say, so say it directly. It's pointless assuming that people know what you think or want. People are poor mind readers; they have no idea what is going on inside you. Save yourself and everybody else, time and trouble by being direct with your feedback.

Make your feedback immediate
If you're concerned, hurt, angry or needing to change something, delaying your communication will often increase these feelings. Over time, smoldering irritation can develop into strong resentment, which can then be

triggered to explode into rage. Immediate communication can quickly solve difficulties and create or improve trust. Here-and-now communications are more effective and exciting and are likely to strengthen relationships.

Make your feedback clear

Clear feedback is a complete and accurate reflection of your observations, thoughts, feelings and needs. Avoid leaving things out, avoid being vague, and avoid being abstract or using jargon. Do not ask questions when you need to make a statement. Keep your feedback congruent, which means the content of the feedback, your tone of voice, your facial expression and your body language, all fit together and say the same thing.

Make your feedback straight

A straight piece of feedback is one in which the stated purpose is identical with the real purpose of the communication. Ask yourself a number of questions:

1. What is it I need to say to this person?
2. Why do I need to say it?
3. What do I want him or her to hear?
4. What do I want him or her to do next?
5. How do I wish similar situations to be in the future?
6. How can I say these clearly for the benefit of us both?

Being straight means being honest, bringing the real agenda into the open, and asking for what you want or need to happen.

Use 'I' statements

Saying how you feel about something, rather than making an accusation, is less likely to create defensiveness in the listener. Saying: 'I feel upset that... I am anxious about... I get concerned when... I wonder what...?' is easier to hear than: 'you didn't... You always... You make me...' etc. Wherever possible, avoid the word 'Why?' as this can make feedback sound like an accusation or an interrogation.

Make your feedback supportive

Ask yourself, 'Do I want my feedback to be heard defensively or accurately?'

The following guidelines could be adhered to and help to avoid the risk of people feeling defensive:
   a. Avoid using labels such as: stupid, selfish, mean, disgusting, worthless, lazy, etc.

b. Avoid making accusations such as: 'You're wrong, you do everything badly, you are a difficult person.'
c. Avoid using sarcasm as it demonstrates contempt.
d. Avoid dragging up past similar situations - to do so might prevent any chance of clarifying how each of you feels about the present situation.
e. Avoid negative comparisons between people: 'you are not as efficient as…'
f. Avoid making judgmental 'you' feedback statements: 'you are… you don't… you never… you always'.
g. Avoid making threats. Making a threat, whether or not you are able or willing to carry it out, is very likely to bring co-operative communication to a screeching halt!

Make your feedback compassionate

It is unlikely that you will know the full extent of what's going on in anyone else's life. Even people you know well might have issues, concerns, thoughts and feelings that they have not disclosed to you. This is even more likely with people you don't know very well or with whom you have only a slight working relationship. There may be reasons about which you know nothing that might be affecting a person's actions and behavior.

Feedback that is given with a sense of compassion is likely to be more effective than feedback that is delivered without any thought to the recipient's feelings.

At the same time you could have some compassion for yourself. It may take some careful thought, self-control and sometimes courage to offer appropriate feedback and bring about the changes or improvement in another person's behavior and actions for the benefit of the group or project.

Offering feedback in these ways can help to avoid win/lose, good/bad, wrong/right situations.

One flowing feedback statement

> It is important to deliver your complete feedback in one flowing statement and without breaks or hesitation.

That way all the elements of the feedback are expressed before the other person has the opportunity to make a response to just one element. Hearing these aspects of the situation from your perspective and your experience will give the person a greater understanding of the bigger picture. This can help them to receive this information without feeling the need to be defensive or to react negatively. It could also help to avoid that person experiencing feelings of hurt or disempowerment.

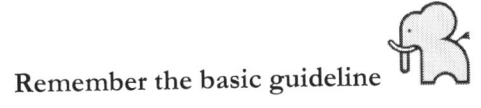

Remember the basic guideline

> Being a constructive communicator is to communicate in the way you would like to be communicated with.

Constructive Communication is described in great detail in three books in this series: SMART TALKING, SMART LISTENING and SMART TALKING & LISTENING TO CHILDREN that are available in paperback and e-book formats from Amazon and accessible through our website: www.youmakethedifference.net/books

3

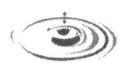

LEADERSHIP

In a group there may be an obvious leader. This might be the person who thought up the group or project. In some groups there might be no obvious leader, although there may be a need for one - at least at the start.

What makes a good leader?

I have asked this question of hundreds of people. Their replies indicate that there are many opinions on the subject:

1. People who are inspirational.
2. People with vision.
3. People with the ideas.
4. People with the drive and enthusiasm to get those ideas off the ground.
5. People with the strategies for success.
6. People with the expertise and experience to make those strategies become reality.
7. People with charisma.
8. People who instill confidence.
9. People who understand how to get the best out of others.
10. People who motivate others to achieve success.
11. People who encourage others by their sheer hard work or dogged determination.

> Although I have met some exceptionally gifted leaders, it is unrealistic to expect all of these qualities to be combined in one individual.

We often have high, sometimes unrealistic expectations of people in leadership roles, which, in my experience, they are almost certain to fail to reach at some time or another. The higher our expectations of leaders, the greater our disappointment in them is likely to be if they fail to meet them. The resulting feelings of disempowerment of the leaders and the disillusionment of the people being led can be painful for all concerned, and may have disastrous consequences for a group.

Voluntary and Community Groups provide many opportunities for people to explore leadership. Having an understanding of what leadership means and how best to manage leadership roles within a group can be empowering for individuals. This understanding might make the difference to the success of a group or whether or not it remains sustainable.

Leadership Myths

There are a number of myths surrounding leadership. As with many myths these might have become a way of explaining things. They may have become part of some people's belief system. For others, these myths can be useful for keeping to the status quo. Some investigation of these myths could prove useful when considering leadership roles within groups.

Myth #1, Leader is another word for 'Boss'

The word leader can bring up a lot of emotions in people. To some people the word, 'leader', represents power or authority. These might be what some people want, some people shy away from having and some people resent in those who have them.

Unfortunate attitudes have developed as a result of how the power of leadership has been used and abused in the past. One of these is the belief that anyone who is egotistical enough to want to be a leader is obviously too egotistical to be trusted with the role.

> I believe that this attitude towards leadership has no place in most groups and it would be wise for the people in them to dispel the myth that leader means boss in their group.

Myth #2, Leaders are born not made

Belief in this myth has allowed people, perceived to be born to lead, to assume leadership roles - whether they are suitable for them or not. Just because a person has some status in society, has been well educated, has been successful in business or has led campaigns or military personnel, does not automatically make them the most appropriate leaders of groups.

This myth can also blind people to their own leadership potential or that of those around them. I have seen this belief prevent the most suitable leadership candidates from stepping forward and the people within a group from recognizing that leadership potential or having the willingness to be led by those people.

From experience it seems to me that natural leaders emerge naturally. The natural leader for any situation will clearly emerge if the conditions are right. Those conditions can be created in a group when there is:

   a. Trust among the group members.
   b. Constructive communication between them.
   c. A recognition and appreciation of the skills and experience within the group.
   d. The willingness of the appropriate people to take a leadership role.
   e. And for the others in the group to support them to do so.

Myth #3, Leaders need to be charismatic

It can be very useful for the initiator of a group or a project to have a charismatic personality. I know of hundreds of projects around the world that only exist because some individuals had the vision, the determination and persistence to initiate them and the charisma to inspire others to join in. Some of these projects are small and local: skateboard parks, animal shelters for example. Others are enormous and global: rainforest protection and regeneration, the feeding of countless starving people. Many of those initiators could be described as charismatic.

However, having a charismatic leader can be a double-edged sword. One edge is that leader's ability to initiate and drive a project; to inspire people and attract the resources needed to maintain it. Just by being who they are, some people have a natural ability to inspire people. Maybe it is their passion for a project, their concern and compassion for others that stirs people into action. Their commitment and dedication might be what encourages loyal support from many people.

The other edge of the sword is the level of dependency that a project can come to have upon that charisma and upon an assumption that other beneficial attributes also exist in that leader. When, along with a charismatic personality, a person has other necessary leadership qualities then a project is likely to benefit and have a great start. In most cases however, it would be wise for those involved in the project, especially the leader, to fully involve other people who have the skills and experience needed to sustain the project.

Charismatic leaders can sometimes be so closely associated with ideas and ideals that it can be difficult to separate one from the other. In many situations this might not matter much. However, if it is perceived that to question one is an automatic attack on the other - whichever way round - this can create problems. There are plenty of examples of this, notably in religious and political movements, past and present. It could be useful for people to have some awareness of this possibility, which might help to avoid charismatic leaders becoming dictators or giving groundless credibility to insubstantial projects, ideas or ideals.

Myth #4, Leaders must be passionate

A passionate and highly motivated leader may be one whose passion for a project is based upon emotion. This emotion may come from some personal experience, such as the illness or the loss of a loved one. It may come from a drive to fight injustice or right a wrong. It may come from a desire to provide care and nurturing to the needy where none exists. It might come from a determination to influence greater sustainability at a local or planetary level.

This passion often sustains levels of energy and enthusiasm in the leader that no other member of the project can match. This might lead to the leaders' resentment of others and to the disempowerment or a sense of inadequacy among the members of the group. It can also encourage the leaders to cut corners or take risks that it is unfair or reasonable to ask others to do.

Remember: An effective passionate leader is one who recognizes that it is unlikely that the other people involved will have the same drive to achieve success for the project as they have, and, who think no less of others because of it!

Myth #5, 'Too many chiefs and not enough Indians.'

This is an old saying in my culture, which, along with another 'Too many cooks spoil the broth', warn against having too many people being involved in making decisions. This myth might apply in groups where there is an absence of agreed decision-making procedures or where the roles within the group are not clearly defined.

> This myth supports the old Paradigm of leaders and followers. In this Paradigm, a leader, or a very small group of people, make the decisions or give instructions, which everyone else involved obeys or carries out. This might have merit in some situations, however this approach is unlikely to prove to be the best method for empowering people in groups.

Myth #6, There is no need for leadership in cooperative groups

This is quite a modern myth, although some traces might be found in some past religious, political and social experiments. To many people this seems to be more of a utopian ideal than a realistic objective. Even so, this ideal could be well worth considering as part of our conscious evolutionary process.

From observation and experience, it seems to me that there are a number of elements essential for enabling 'leaderless' cooperative groups to function well and be effective:

1. Understanding and agreement of the purpose and objectives of the group by everyone involved.
2. Commitment to these, outweighing any personal opinions or needs, by everyone in the group.
3. Thorough understanding of the function of each member, their dedication to that function and the full support of the other members of the group.
4. Constant attention to group cohesion and the development of the group culture.
5. Willingness for regular review and reflection.
6. Genuine cooperative decision-making.
7. Full engagement in any required transformation processes.
8. Allegiance by everyone involved to the decisions made by the group.

For all of these elements to be in place would require a group made up of quite enlightened people. I have learned that very few of us are as enlightened as we imagine ourselves to be.

There have been groups that have had some degree of success in establishing these elements. Even so, they have discovered that a huge amount of attention needs to be given to group processing and many things can take a long time to achieve while doing so. This can result in inadequate attention being paid to other important issues such as acquiring and management of resources, the wellbeing of the members and the improvement of technical skills and equipment needed to function in an ever-changing world.

With so much attention focused on internal processing, a leaderless group can become self-absorbed and less interested or effective in relating to people outside the group. The result can be elitism, a sense of superiority over people whose approaches are different or considered by the group to be inferior. This could be self-defeating to a group whose stated objectives are to be of service to others or to be a model of inspiration.

I have noticed that much of the success of a seemingly leaderless group depends upon their reasons for being leaderless. In some groups, the reason has resulted from the group having experienced an authoritarian leader for a while and being determined to prevent any individual from having that level of power again. This has sometimes left these groups floundering around directionless for some time.

> Fear or suspicion of any form of leadership can itself become a form of tyranny, which dis-empowers people and prevents appropriate leaders from emerging.

Even so, in some groups the reason for wanting to be leaderless is a genuine desire for cooperative working and commitment to the mutual empowerment of all those involved. In these groups, each member will be encouraged by and will encourage and support fellow members to step into any leadership role, whenever their skills and experience are what are needed.

Effective self-managing groups

> Voluntary and Community Groups provide the opportunity for people to turn this leaderless myth on its head. Rather than being a leaderless group, a group could be self-managing and made up of people taking leadership roles when appropriate or necessary.

Each of the members might embody one or more of the attributes of a good leader and so between them they would have all those aspects covered. The elements needed for an effective leaderless group, as previously described, would be essential; as would each member being committed to taking on the leadership role in his or her field of expertise and experience when required; and when each member of the group encourages and supports one another to do so.

This type of self-managing group might still feel the need for someone to hold the overall vision and to help members to keep aligned with it. It could be beneficial to have someone with facilitation skills to manage meetings and discussions, to coordinate communications among members and to disseminate information. Within such a group there may be a requirement for people to coordinate teams. Some functions and activities of a group might need people with experience to direct operations. Whatever any of these functions are called in any group - these are leadership roles.

Leadership Styles

There are a variety of leadership styles, each having benefits and disadvantages and each being appropriate for particular situations. Some are more effective than others and it seems that a leadership style is often an extension of that leader's personality. These styles fall broadly into one of the following categories: authoritarian, democratic, facilitating.

Authoritarian Leadership

Authoritarian leaders lead from the top down and might be dictatorial towards their group members. They can be rigid in their thinking and may be difficult to deal with, especially when they are disagreed with.

There are other attributes that often come along with authoritarian leadership and might hold a project back from reaching its full potential. These characteristics might include: pride, self-importance, self-righteousness and a sense of superiority. These can result in a number of situations:

a. The leader's unwillingness or inability to listen to the advice and ideas of others.
b. Their unwillingness to delegate functions and decision-making to others.
c. Their lack of patience and tolerance that might undermine or disempower group members, workers and volunteers.
d. Their inability to recognize their own lack of good communication skills.
e. Their inability to inspire good communications within the project or group.
f. Their unrealistically high assessment of their own skills and abilities.
g. Their low opinion of the skills and abilities of the other people involved.

Authoritarianism is sometimes confused with strong leadership, which, in my experience, it rarely is. In fact, any need a leader might have to be dictatorial, to get their own way or to bully people into submission could be based upon their insecurities and the fear that these insecurities will be exposed. There is nothing strong in that.

However, an authoritarian style of leadership - preferably without the negative attributes - might be vital in critical or dangerous situations where people need to be clearly guided or instructed in what to do. This style might be useful in the very early stages of getting a project off the ground.

Democratic Leadership

Democratic leaders are likely to delegate many of the leadership responsibilities to others in the group. They will work with those involved to set up systems and structures to empower the members. They will solicit proposals, encourage discussion, and include as many people as is feasible in decision-making. Within the group, the majority rules most of the time, although, this type of leader might occasionally exercise their veto during voting.

Democratic leadership is most applicable for encouraging cooperation and creating a culture that will support positive group development.

Facilitating Leadership

Some leaders seem hardly to be leaders at all. They appear to have very little formal influence upon most aspects of the group's activities, which they trust to be handled by the people who have taken responsibility for them. They facilitate group discussion and decision-making and are likely to choose to forego any power of veto.

Facilitating leadership is most suitable when a group has reached the cooperative stage in its development and those in the group have confidence and trust in themselves and in one another. Involvement from these leaders will then mostly be supportive and encouraging to members of the group as they carry out their tasks.

Each of these three styles will be suitable for specific circumstances.

Appropriate Leadership

Appropriate leadership is just that - the appropriate style of leadership for the circumstances.

An appropriate leadership style is sometimes determined by timing. Getting a project off the ground may require some authoritarian leadership at the beginning. New projects, new organizations even new countries can benefit from a short period of benign authoritarian style of leadership. However, that is likely to only be effective for a while and will become unnecessary when co-operation and democratic decision-making are developed.

To develop group cohesion and cooperation, to build trust, to create openness and clear communication within a group will require a leadership style that is democratic, supportive and encouraging.

A self-managing group, functioning within a culture of cooperation and mutual respect, could then enjoy the benefits of a facilitating style of leadership.

The positive aspects of each of these styles can be implemented as needed or appropriate. For example:

1. When in charge of volunteers entering specific data into the computer a group or team leader might be authoritarian when instructing them how to carry out that task; there is no room for discussion, just a right and a wrong way to do it.
2. A leader might be democratic in discussions with their volunteer team on how to keep the phones manned over a period of time, such as the holiday season. He or she might explain what needs to happen and then discusses with them how this can be done to best suit everyone concerned. The team could then sort out a Rota or vote upon who will work the phones, and when. The team leader might veto an unrealistic plan; however, their intent would be to support whatever the team comes up with.
3. A leader might facilitate a group discussion about fundraising or ideas for new projects. In most cases it would be inappropriate for them to have more or less a say about these than anyone else in the group, especially those who have expertise. The appropriate members of the group would step up to take on the responsibility for implementing these ideas and projects. In this, as in many other situations, a facilitating leader would confidently trust their group colleagues to support one another in achieving the agreed aims.

It is possible for a person who has significant self-awareness and an understanding of group development to lead a group through all of the stages of its development. It seems to me that this is what Nelson Mandela managed to achieve in a country poised for civil war when he became leader; so this ought not to be impossible to achieve within a small voluntary group intending to be helpful within its community!

Your choice

If you are the leader of a group, a team, a project or an activity, you may have already developed your leadership style or have a preference for one of them over the others. It might serve you and your group to consider if this choice is the most appropriate for the time and circumstances.

Q Some useful questions to consider:
   a. Is this a conscious choice of leadership style or extension of your personality?
   b. Is your choice of leadership style based on your needs or on the needs of the group?
   c. What kind of leadership style might your project or group really need at this time?
   d. Would your leadership style benefit from some flexible thinking?

A group being led along traditional lines might find it beneficial for the whole group to consider these questions regarding leadership. This is not intended to undermine any current leadership; it is to expand the group's awareness of leadership options.

> The key to choosing an appropriate leadership style for any situation is an awareness of the circumstances: the stage a group has reached in its development; sensitivity to the needs of the group; the characteristics of potential leaders and flexibility to choose accordingly.

Being a leader

So far we've been concentrating upon the leadership roles of management and function. There are other aspects of leadership that impact the effectiveness and sustainability of any group. These aspects are about influencing the attitudes and behavior of fellow members and the culture of the group. This form of leadership is more about demonstrating cooperative and supportive ways of being and modeling the attitudes, behavior and methods of personal communication that inspires others and encourages group cohesion. It includes a willingness to take responsibility, not only for a function or an activity, also for one's thoughts, words and deeds and the consequences of any of these.

The seven C's of leadership

For this kind of leadership to be most effective it would be useful to consider the Five C's of leadership:
   1. Commitment.
   2. Creativity.

3. Communication.
4. Collaboration.
5. Co-operation.
6. Consensus.
7. Courage.

Commitment

Leadership and commitment go hand-in-hand. Leadership commitment means not only saying you are committed to a principle, to a cause, to an outcome, to a way of doing things or to a group of people; it requires a demonstration of that commitment. If you are not seen to be committed to the cause, to the goals of the group, to the outcome of a project or to the people you are working with, then how can you expect others to be?

> Showing commitment to any of these is a demonstration of leadership.

Creativity

Leadership often requires creative thinking. Whether that is thinking laterally, thinking outside the box, recognizing options and opportunities or encouraging creative thinking in others.

> These aspects of creative thinking are demonstrations of leadership.

Communication

Effective leadership depends upon effective communication. Whether that is delivering instructions; succinctly getting ideas across; clearly stating the reality of a situation or encouraging and supporting the constructive communication of other people.

> Being a good communicator in any of these areas is a demonstration of leadership.

Collaboration

This form of leadership means working collaboratively with people in the team, perhaps bringing people together in groups to work in mutual support of one another or seeking collaboration from people outside the group or organization.

> A person able to inspire collaboration with and from others is demonstrating leadership.

Co-operation

Empowering leadership inspires cooperative working. The leader who does not work cooperatively with people in their team is likely to be more of a dictator than a leader. A leader who does not seek cooperation from those outside of the group may lead the group into a place of isolation and alienation from those whose support would be helpful or necessary.

> A person who is able to encourage and maintain co-operation within a group and/or is able to attract cooperation from others outside of the group is demonstrating leadership.

Consensus

Leadership does not mean making all the decisions. Inspiring, supportive and empowering leadership results from ensuring that those who will carry out decisions have had a hand in making them, preferably through Consensus.

> A person encouraging and/or facilitating consensus decision making in a group is demonstrating leadership.

Courage

It often takes courage to be a leader. It can require courage to take on a role, to stand up and be counted or to say the things that need to be said when mindful of the potential consequences. It may need courage to take on responsibility. Especially if you are the only person to recognize there is some responsibility to take; if you might not be perceived as the obvious person to take it; or when others are unable or unwilling to do so.

> The willingness to step forward in any of these circumstances is a demonstration of leadership.

Everyone is a potential leader

This is not just warm and fuzzy language! It is my belief based upon decades of experience.

> It seems obvious that in any situation the person with the appropriate skills, the appropriate information and/or experience; who has the appropriate attitude and intention and is willing to step forward at the appropriate time, is the obvious leader in that situation.

Whether or not the obvious person takes up any leadership role in a situation is usually dependent upon their **courage, confidence and willingness** to pick up the leadership baton at that time, and, whether the people they would be leading are willing to allow them to do so.

Being courageous

It may take courage for a person to offer himself or herself as a leader in a situation. Especially if they are new to a group or if there is significant or obvious difference between them and the other members, such as age, gender, ethnic background, religion etc. A potential leader might be concerned that any action they would recommend might be unpopular with the rest of the group. If a person has seen others who have put themselves forward for leadership being metaphorically shot at, it may take great courage for them to risk putting themselves in the same position.

Being confident

For most of us, confidence in our abilities and in ourselves in general can take a long time to develop and yet can so quickly be undermined. I have seen talented people join groups with the very best of intentions, only to find their confidence in their abilities being eroded by the judgmental culture of the group and the critical and unsupportive attitudes of the members.

In some groups it may take a lot of self-confidence for some people to offer their skills, knowledge or experience, especially in those groups which have a blame culture, where there is little mutual trust and loyalty or where the word 'leader' is assumed to mean boss.

If the group is unaware of the three stages of group development and/or the whole group or some members are stuck at the assertion stage, then the appropriate leaders for any situation are unlikely to be able to easily emerge.

Being willing

The willingness to take the responsibility for leadership is what makes someone **into** a leader even if it's only for a short while or in particular circumstances.

Developing leadership strengths

Developing the leadership qualities of courage, confidence and willingness is essential personal development work. And, although it sometimes might be hard work, the rewards can be so great that every moment and every bit of effort is well worthwhile.

This work requires three things:
1. To know what you want to achieve.
2. The opportunities to practice.
3. The support and encouragement of at least one other person.

What do you want to achieve?

Perhaps they are some of the following:
a. Start a group or move a project forward.
b. Gain confidence and have the courage to offer ideas and suggestions.
c. Propose processes or actions.
d. Speak up in meetings.
e. Challenge existing ways of doing things or other people's ideas, perceptions or assumptions.

The opportunities to practice

Many of your everyday conversations can offer chances to practice communicating clearly and to try out strategies for getting ideas across, and for respectfully challenging statements or situations about which you have concerns. The group you are currently with could perhaps offer you plenty of opportunities to practice your courage and confidence in these areas.

However, if your previous experience with this group has been particularly uncomfortable or difficult, you might consider joining another group, maybe for a while, to flex your courage and confidence muscles in a new or more supportive setting.

Seeking support

You could seek the support and encouragement of a mentor or a coach. If neither of these is available to you, then find someone who would be willing to engage with you in mutual peer support. This could be someone in the same group or someone who has no involvement in it. You might find a person who is struggling with some of the same issues as yourself.

You could perhaps find somebody who, although dealing with entirely different issues, would value some mutual support.

Doing the work

The moves forward in developing yourself and your leadership skills need only be made in tiny steps. No giant leaps are needed or recommended.

Take a small step in one of the areas in which you wish to improve and see how it feels. Notice the response from others and then get some feedback from your support person or people. If something works well, do more of it. If something doesn't work well, do something different next time. If something you do feels too uncomfortable, explore with your support person why that might be. It could be just that the step you have taken was a bit too big at this point.

Practice makes perfect

In any area of development, the trick is to keep on keeping on. This is why the support of others is so valuable. It can prevent you from feeling alone and vulnerable and from doubting yourself, giving up or slipping into a decline if things don't go so well.

With practice, your levels of courage, confidence and willingness will grow. You will probably begin to wonder why you ever had any doubts in yourself or your leadership abilities. You may find yourself effortlessly assuming leadership roles, perhaps small at first, and then, with increased confidence, roles with greater potential for making a difference. This may all be so seamless that people may not notice. If they do notice and remark upon it, by then you will have enough confidence to deal with whatever comes up.

Supportive leadership

> For a group, team or activity leader in a Voluntary or Community Group to be most effective, he or she, would be wise to use more elements of mentoring than managing, and place a greater emphasis on facilitation and upon coaching than upon controlling.

Such groups are usually made up of volunteers who are offering their time, skills and expertise in support of the group or project and for the benefit of others. The people in these groups thrive on encouragement and mutual respect. When people feel recognized for their abilities and trusted to use those abilities effectively they are more likely to continue to do so than when feeling doubted, distrusted overly managed or controlled.

These groups are likely to be less than effective when attitudes of criticism and disrespect lead to feelings of disempowerment among the group members. This also applies to negative attitudes, which can be harmful to the survival of a group. Negative attitudes could include: defeatism, aggression, undermining, sabotaging and the seeking of scapegoats. Attitudes that would be helpful in a group situation are: Cooperation, open-mindedness, honest and direct communication and compassion.

Timing

> An important part of being an effective leader is the comprehension of right timing.

Understanding the timing of strategies. Knowing when it is the right time to initiate a discussion or a process. Understanding the appropriate times to intervene or to hold back.

There are likely to be times when changes need to be made to the structure to fulfill the objectives of the project or even to guarantee its survival. Any inability on the part of the leader to recognize when the project has grown to the point where major changes are necessary could serious restrict the projects potential.

This understanding of timing includes knowing when it is time to release the reins of leadership into the hands of someone else.

Loyalty and leadership

Wise leaders know to place loyalty high on the group's agenda for achievement, and they set the example for loyalty within their group. They demonstrate loyalty at every opportunity: to the project, to the group's principles and agreements and most especially to every group member. Through this example, loyalty can become automatic among group members and an intrinsic part of the group culture.

Criticism of and jokes about the leader might be commonplace within groups of people who feel unhappy with a leader's decisions or disempowered by that person's style of leadership. Although this behavior might relieve feelings of frustration and even create some solidarity within the group, nonetheless, it is an example of disloyalty. It is even more so if those criticisms and jokes are taken outside of the group. At the end of the day, how will this help? This type of behavior might do more damage to the group's effectiveness and success than the actions of the leader being criticized.

It seems to me that within Voluntary and Community Groups there is no place for the 'us' and 'them' attitudes of separation that exist in many hierarchical structures. This sense of separation easily allows for blame to be placed on the 'others'. Voluntary and Community Groups, Organizations and Associations thrive on the belief that, 'we are all in this together'. Everyone in a group can contribute towards this sense of togetherness.

It may take a lot of courage for a group to bring their concerns and distress about the quality of leadership to the notice of the leader, especially an authoritarian leader, and yet it might be difficult for the group to be effective or even to survive if this is not done.

There are a number of ways in which concerns of this nature can be brought out into the open. The choice of which will depend upon the make-up of the group, how communications within the group are conducted and the personality of the leader:

Options:
   a. Concerns can be brought up in regular group meetings.
   b. A special meeting could be called in which they can be presented.
   c. A small number of people could be delegated to have a discussion with the leader.
   d. One person who is trusted by the leader or who is likely to be listened to by him or her could have a quiet word in private with the leader. A useful formula for having a quiet word by creating a 'Complete Message' is described in a later chapter.

If the situation is such that no one feels able to be part of any of these verbal presentations then the group might consider composing a letter to the leader that, in non-confrontational language, clearly describes the concerns of the group. Within it there would be a request for a meeting to discuss these issues. Depending on the circumstances the meeting could be between all the members of the group and the leader or between him or her and representatives of the group.

In any of the choices of meeting it might be wise for the group to obtain the services of an independent facilitator or even a mediator.

Two or three options of dates and times could be suggested in the letter from which the leader can choose. This letter ought to be signed by everyone in the group if possible. Even though communication is often done most easily through e-mails these days, e-mails can be easily overlooked, unintentionally or otherwise, in a busy inbox. It would seem wise practice for this to be a paper letter in a sealed envelope and perhaps placed upon the leader's desk.

You can make the difference through leadership

You could be an example of leadership that would offer encouragement to others to find or develop their leadership qualities. It can often just take one person to make a significant difference to a group by doing something different, to take the initiative, to speak up, to ask a question, to make a suggestion, to be positive and supportive.

Make a note

Make a note of all the areas in which you could demonstrate leadership in your group.

> It often only takes one person to show the way for a group to consist of people who are willing to take responsibility for making things happen, who are able to step into appropriate leadership roles whenever necessary while having the support and confidence of the other members, and to encourage others to do the same. This is leadership.

4

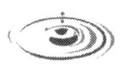

FORMING GROUPS

> The urge to gather together in groups seems fundamental to being human.

This is what has allowed us to evolve into societies that function reasonably well for most citizens. And yet, in many places, increasingly over the past half-century, there seems to have developed a culture of individuality in which ever greater numbers of people seem to have pursued their desires and goals alone, sometimes without much thought to how the outcomes might impact others. Now, however, many people are recognizing the numerous benefits of being in groups in some areas of their lives.

Being in a group provides the following:
- Ready access to other people's skills and experience.
- Mutual support.
- Encouragement.
- Companionship and shared enjoyment.
- Working in groups is often the easiest way to achieve success.

Some groups seemed to form themselves as people gather naturally around a common interest, a mutual need or an inspiring idea.

On some occasions the idea for a project comes first and a group is created to achieve the project's purpose. At other times a group is formed first, whose members then initiate a project through which they can be of service.

Common interest and support groups

People form themselves into groups for reasons as diverse as meditation and attending international sporting events, flower arranging and skydiving, local hospice care and providing international aid.

Clubs, teams and associations are all versions of groups. Even the most competitive of individuals who are totally focused upon their own goals will usually fare better in a group that offers support. Although it is common for groups to form around projects or activities such as sports or hobbies, there are many other reasons for people to gather. One of these reasons is for mutual support.

Comfort and strength can be gained from being in a support group and sharing some of life's challenges with other people who are dealing with similar circumstances or shared experiences.

Such groups have proven to be very beneficial to those wishing to lose weight, be a better parent or to stop smoking. Being part of such groups can relieve feelings of isolation, loneliness and helplessness that often come along with issues concerning health, relationships, finances and recovery from such things as loss, trauma, abuse and addiction.

Many of these self-help, support and recovery groups are local chapters of national or international voluntary organizations that have a common structure and formula that has proven to be effective. Professional practitioners and experienced people usually lead these groups that will often have been created by people who have been helped by such groups and now want to be of assistance to others facing the same difficulties that they have dealt with.

> Anyone starting up such a group is likely to receive support and encouragement from similar groups elsewhere and to benefit from having clear, tried and trusted procedures to follow to achieve success in supporting people and sustaining the group.

Due to the need to provide confidentiality and anonymity for their members many of these groups do not show up on the radar of Voluntary and Community Groups. Even so, they provide an invaluable service, not only to their members, also to the communities in which they operate.

Mutual Support Groups

There is a growing recognition for other types of support groups within communities. Some of the most valuable are Mutual Support Groups for those people involved in creating or sustaining projects intended to achieve the vision that a community has for its future.

People coming together in Mutual Support Groups can benefit from opportunities to share with others what is working well for them in their projects, what is not going so well and how this is impacting their intent for their project.

> Being able to think out loud in a supportive group about the next steps to take towards possible solutions can often dispel feelings of overwhelm or despair.

The structure and guidelines for Mutual Support Groups are described in detail in two books: EFFORTLESS FACILITATION and EMPOWERING VOLUNTEER MANAGEMENT in the MAKING THE DIFFERENCE series which are available in paperback and e-book format from Amazon and are accessible through our website: www.youmakethedifference.net/books

Being together

What seems rarely acknowledged is the wish that some people have for just being together with others. For such a group to be enjoyable and effective there is no need for the members to have anything in common other than a desire to be part of a group. However, it often transpires that there will be threads of commonality that weave through such a group.

For example:

One such group that I belonged to for many years started out as a group of women over a certain age who wanted to hang out together. We had no agenda other than being together and sharing whatever highlights or challenges in our lives that we chose to communicate to one another. For years we met once a month for several hours, either in one another's homes or on a visit to a place of interest, during which times we had a meal together.

The similarities that emerged within this group were: we all lived alone or at some distance from our families, we had all led, and a couple of us still led, very busy lives. Most of us had experienced and survived physical challenges, debilitating illnesses or life-threatening conditions and we all enjoyed good food.

The strongest thread that held us together was our understanding of the importance of spending time **being** rather than **doing**. Of taking time to be with people we liked and respected and having no need, if only for a few hours, to do anything profitable, constructive, meaningful or useful. Many of us had been involved in voluntary hospice work, which we knew had strengthened our awareness of and deepened our commitment to conscious living as well as conscious dying. We called ourselves 'The Being Group'.

Project Groups

Projects can be launched and brought to fruition by passionate, competent individuals working alone who might choose to do so because their project is small or it is only the skills and experience of that one person which are being offered.

Many people prefer to work independently of others for some reason. Maybe they do not know of appropriate people with whom to engage or are unsure of how to attract supporters to their project. Perhaps they have been let down by people in the past and now do not have enough confidence in the quality of other people's commitment. They might feel uncomfortable in groups, which is understandable if past experiences of being in groups have been unsatisfactory or unpleasant.

However, there are so many advantages for community projects to be managed by community groups that I encourage anyone with a project idea to seek out others with whom to work. The information in this book is offered to help groups to be effective and to support one another to enjoy the experience of being in a group.

Sometimes people form a group and then look for a project to work with. Perhaps they are attracted to one that already exists or the idea for one that has been decided upon. People who work with one another professionally might look for a project to support or initiate. This might be a group of people working in a business or pupils in a school. It could also be those in a group who have successfully completed one project and are seeking another one in which to continue to work together.

If such groups do not have a project then engaging in an 'Action Search' process could be helpful for identifying a suitable idea. This process is described in the book EFFORTLESS FACILITATION in the MAKING THE DIFFERENCE series available in paperback and e-book format from Amazon and accessible through our website: www.youmakethedifference.net/books

Forming a project group

An ideal project group would be one in which every skill required is provided by experienced people who get along well with each other and are all committed to the project's objectives. This is not an unrealistic ideal! There are a number of ways that people have suggested to achieve this:

1. Have a clear intention for the project and trust that the right people will turn up.
2. Gather together a group of people who know and like each other, who believe that the project is a good idea and who are willing to learn the skills necessary for the project's success.
3. Seek out the people whose skills and experience would make the project successful, inspire them to work on the project and hope that they get along with one another sufficiently well to work cooperatively together.

In my experience it can work to do all three while paying attention to forming the group culture and methods for creating and maintaining cooperation.

Implementing the following processes will create a firm foundation upon which to build a group project:

Intention

Have a clear intention. Commitment has magic in it; and so does strong intention. I have seen things materialize, seemingly effortlessly, purely from the intention of a strong-minded individual or group. However, it would seem wise to support a strong intention with some sensible strategic planning and pro-activity.

Visualization

Have a clear vision for what you want to achieve and then imagine achieving it. Make the image of success bright, colorful, exciting, interesting, and enjoyable. See the people you want to be involved happily, cooperatively and effectively engaged in achieving the objectives. Hold onto this vision through thick and thin and embellish it from time to time. As each stage of success is accomplished, celebrate that success.

The Ideal Day exercise in the EFFORTLESS FACILITATION and EMPOWERING VOLUNTEER MANAGEMENT already mentioned could help with this visualization process, which can be done alone or with others.

Identify the appropriate people

Identify the skills and experience that are needed for the project's success. Seek out the most appropriate people and invite them to join the project group. Some of those people might be known to you and may already be good friends with you and/or with one another.

> Supportive, encouraging and positive people are invaluable in any group.

SUCCESSFUL GROUPS & PROJECTS

Be inclusive

It may seem that a group formed of nice, friendly people who you know well and who like one another would make up the ideal group to work together harmoniously and cooperatively. However, no matter how pleasant the prospect may be of being in a group with friends, if they do not have the knowledge and experience needed then this might not result in the best outcome for the project.

When creating an effective project group it will be the appropriate skills, experience, contacts and essential qualities in members that are needed.

There may be some skills that you know to be essential to the project's success and you do not know anyone with those skills. Find out who has them! Ask around! Talk it over with the people already committed to the project. Put the word out in your community. Some great networking is done amongst Voluntary and Community Groups and somebody in these networks will know just the people you need to approach to join your group.

Some of the people whose skills, experience or contacts you recognize would be useful to the project may be total strangers. Ask them to join the group anyway. People will say either yes or no. They may have personal reasons for saying no, such as time restraints, or they may not fully understand your vision or recognize the need for the project. Respect their decision. Even if they say no now, they may say yes later, when the project is more established.

It could save time and effort to develop a clear strategy for attracting group members for use in the future when there will probably be an ongoing need for new members to replace those who leave or to help with an expansion of work. The strategy options for attracting volunteers set out in EMPOWERING VOLUNTEER MANAGEMENT would be helpful.

Create an open group

Openness is an antidote to secrets and misinformation, to restricted thinking and to feelings of separation and elitism.

The most effective groups are open in their communication with one another and with those outside the group. They are open to suggestions, to new ideas and new or different ways of doing things. They are also open to other people joining the group at any time, who have the skills, experience, contacts or attitudes that would be beneficial.

> It is my experience that groups are most effective when there is commitment, clear intention, careful planning, sensible thinking, direct requests for what is needed and openness to possibilities.

5

DEVELOPING THE GROUP CULTURE

Understanding Groups in chapter one offers a lot of information on the evolution of group culture and the stages any group is likely to go through in its development. Because the quality of relationships within a group is greatly determined by the quality of communication between its members, this subject is also covered in some detail in a later chapter.

Establishing Values & Ethics

It is vital for a group to be clear about what values and ethics will underpin the work. Going through this process can be a useful way to discover the common ground or the differences between group members.

People will have different priorities or personal agendas, which will influence or be influenced by their personal values and ethics. If people have been drawn together in a common cause, there is most likely to be enough similar threads of values and ethics among them that can be woven into an agreement to build the foundations of their work and to hold them together.

If, at the start of a group coming together, processes are gone through to identify the group's values and ethics, this will go a long way towards bringing inclusion and cohesion to the group. This activity might be the most important work to establish the group and support its sustainability.

Having said that, it is never too late for an established group to identify and make agreements about their shared values and ethics. Some of the processes useful for this can be found in the books: ENJOYABLE & EFFECTIVE MEETINGS and in EFFORTLESS FACILITATION in this series.

> Although there will be specific values and ethics required for each group to effectively achieve its aims, there are a number that would be beneficial in any group: mutual respect, honesty, clarity, straightforwardness, tolerance, cooperation, taking responsibility, and willingness.

When these underpin the attitudes, communication, behavior and actions of individuals and the group as a whole, that group is unlikely to go far wrong.

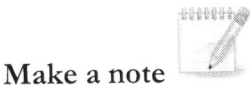

Make a note

Make a note of the values and ethics that you would like to see established in your group.

Making Agreements

When the values and ethics of the group are identified and decided upon by everyone involved, these could form the basis of a Group Agreement. Whether called Agreement, Intention, Commitment, Statement of Common Ground or anything else, this can be a great aid to maintaining cohesion, congruency and trust within the group.

The following example of a group agreement has been adapted from the Statement of Common Ground, devised many years ago in the Findhorn Community. This has proved to be a useful template for the agreements of many groups and organizations.

Group Agreement
1. Support
I wholeheartedly support the aims of this group and the wellbeing and ongoing development of all group members - including myself.
2. Personal integrity and respect
I will maintain high standards of personal integrity, embodying congruence of thought, word and action. I will respect other people, their

views, origins, backgrounds, issues and experiences.

3. Direct communication

I will use clear and honest communication with straightforwardness, attentive listening and respectful responses. In public and in private I will avoid speaking in any way that maligns or demeans others. I will talk **to** people rather than **about** them and will not seek to gossip or collude. I will challenge any actions, manipulation or intimidation that I feel may be detrimental to myself or to others.

4. Responsibility

I will take full responsibility for my thoughts, words and actions. I am willing to listen to constructive criticism and to offer constructive feedback to others in a caring and appropriate fashion that will support each to grow. I acknowledge that there may be wider perspectives than my own and deeper concerns than those that immediately affect me. I will take responsibility to work through or put aside my personal issues for the benefit of the whole group.

5. Conflict resolution

I will make every effort to resolve all personal and group conflict as soon as possible. In the event of a dispute continuing unresolved I will adhere to the group grievance procedure or I may call for an advocate, friend, independent observer or mediator to support a mediated process.

6. Cooperation

I will work cooperatively within the group and consider other people's views carefully and respectfully. I recognize that others may make decisions that affect me and I agree to respect the care, integrity and wisdom that they have put into the decision-making process.

7. Commitment

I commit to keeping these agreements and to exercising the spirit of this statement in all my dealings.

Signature.

Date.

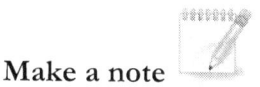

Make a note

Make a note of the elements you would like to see included in agreements made in your group.

Challenging broken agreements

When a group has created a statement of values and ethics that each member has agreed or committed to, then anyone in the group will be in a position to challenge any other member whose behavior demonstrates a disregard for those values and ethics.

> The challenging of a person regarding their agreement can be more effective than directly challenging their behavior and certainly more supportive than making criticism or judgments.

Q

'**How does this help?**' is a useful question to ask a group member whose behavior is outside the agreed parameters of the group's values and ethics. You might also say something like:

'I notice the way you have been speaking to people does not seem to fit with your agreement to be respectful in your communications. Can you find other ways to say what you want to and keep to your agreements?'

Meetings

Much of the work and many of the activities in groups take place in meetings. In my experience, the quality of group meetings can determine how successful a group or a project will be. It is for this reason that the first books to be published in the MAKING THE DIFFERENCE series were on meetings.

A detailed and in-depth study of all aspects of meetings can be found in ENJOYABLE & EFFECTIVE MEETINGS. This book offers guidelines for participation in and for the management of several types of meetings. It includes information on essential procedures, methods for decision-making, on many useful processes and how to use them in tricky situations.

Included in the second book, EFFORTLESS FACILITATION, are suggestions for designing and planning facilitated meetings and events, information on methods, procedures and processes, and insights into making facilitation effortless. There are also some ready-made meeting designs that could be adapted for many situations. Both of these books are in paperback and e-book versions and available from Amazon and our website: www.youmakethedifference.net/books

> You could make an enormous difference to your group by helping to develop a supportive and efficient meeting culture.

When things go wrong in groups

Some of the things that can go wrong will be specific to each group and other things will be general and applicable to most groups.

Having awareness

It would be beneficial to any group to have awareness of the things that could go wrong:

a. Some problems within groups may be practical ones such as lack of funding or other resources – including people; changes to regulations or alteration of requirements.

b. Some problems escalate when there is insufficient knowledge and experience within the group for dealing with unforeseen difficulties and unexpected situations.

c. Some problems within groups result from the ways in which the members behave towards one another. Conflicts might be inevitable if people have not developed Constructive Communication skills. Cooperation and group cohesion might be threatened if there is a lack of understanding of the stages of the group's development or adequate attention has not been paid to the evolution of the culture of the group, particularly in reference to the behavior of its members.

d. Some difficulties arise from inappropriate leadership or/and unwillingness among group members to take responsibility, both for their roles within the group and for their personal behavior.

Ways to handle many of these difficulties might be found by returning to the chapter on Understanding Groups; looking to see which elements are missing or have been ignored; and considering how to now introduce them into the group. To have strategies in place for group creative thinking and developing ideas will help the group to be positively proactive rather than negatively alarmed.

It could be helpful for the group to have access to an experienced group facilitator at times like these.

Remember: It is a wise group that has strategies in place for when things do go wrong – which they almost certainly will do from time to time.

Reviews

Prevention is better than cure! By having awareness of what could detrimentally affect the dynamics within the group, these difficulties might be avoided. A useful strategy to pursue is that of having regular reviews to identify what is working well within the project and what is not.

Spring Cleaning

Sometimes a group or an organization is so busy getting on with the work, coping with insufficient funding or lack of workers and helpers, that not enough time, if any, is devoted to morale or dealing with the small things that irritate or upset people and make work or working relationships difficult.

This can create problems, because, to use a couple of clichés: most people tend **not** to suffer in silence, and, misery loves company. Gripes and complaints can become the basis for a ground swell of discontent and negative thinking. This can undermine the effectiveness of the group or project; turn working relationships sour and can create an atmosphere that nobody wants to be in.

> Attitudes within a group or an organization can become tarnished by unresolved small concerns and niggling complaints. It can be useful to devote a meeting to giving these an airing and finding solutions to them.

The Spring Cleaning method is effective for this as it begins with a Brainstorming session to bring problems out into the open. Although Brainstorming is usually seen as a way of generating positive ideas; it can also be a useful way to get out into the open all the things that are not working well or those that people in a group feel unhappy about. Because it's not always easy to recognize who is saying what in a Brainstorming session, it allows a certain amount of anonymity and safety for people to say the things they may not feel able to openly express in other circumstances.

I have named this process Spring Cleaning because of its potential result and because it is an effective way of starting a new year in the life of a group or an organization, whether this is the calendar year or following after the Annual General Meeting.

> This Spring Cleaning process is metaphorically throwing open the doors and windows of the daily workings of the group or organization, sweeping out the dust of accumulated grumbles, putting the shine back on individual and group attitudes and freshening up the air of mutual support and cooperation.

A simple version of this process can be held at any time when it is noticed that small issues are building up or when the harmony of the group is out of whack.

Facilitation

This could be a process that would benefit from being managed by an outside facilitator. If facilitation is handled from within the group, a main facilitator could manage the process, a co-facilitator could pay attention to the morale and wellbeing of the group and a third person could do the scribing. This will share the load and the responsibility and allow each of those people time to also participate in the process.

Naming the meeting

It is important that as many people as possible in the group or organization attend this meeting. In having a title such as: **'How can we improve?'** along with a subtitle such as: **'your opportunity to have all your concerns heard'**, it can be surprising how many people, who may not normally like to attend meetings, will flock to this one!

Inclusive meetings

The guidelines for creating inclusive meetings found in the book ENJOYABLE & EFFECTIVE MEETINGS or in EFFORTLESS FACILITATION could assist in ensuring that as many of the appropriate people as possible attend. If this process is conducted within a large organization make sure there is proper representation of every department in order to bring all necessary perspectives to the meeting. It could be sensible to first run the process separately in each department; any organization-wide issues arising could then be brought to another meeting of representatives of these departments.

Stating the intention

Begin with a clear statement of the intention of the Spring Clean. Something like: 'We intend to bring into the open for discussion and resolution those large and small issues that are getting in the way of this being a happy, cooperative and productive group'.

Breaking the ice and creating the atmosphere

Have some activities that can help to break the ice, reconnect people with one another, improve trust and increase energy levels. Such an activity could be the ice breaking game. The useful Guide to Group Games is available to download for free from our website: www.youmakethedifference.net.

The Brainstorming

Go through the steps in a Brainstorming process. (If this is unfamiliar to you, this process is described in EFFORTLESS FACILITATION.) Encourage everyone to shout out something that irritates, annoys, disappoints or disempowers him or her in his or her experience of the group or organization/project. These are written on a flip chart or board.

The objective at this stage is to identify the areas of concern - the things that are not working well; rather than individual behavior. There is a need to be very clear that this is not an opportunity to accuse or to blame individuals. No individuals are to be named and no accusations are to be made. If these are shouted out they are not to be written up and the facilitator can ask for that contribution to be reworded.

If there is some reticence from the participants, the facilitator could ask some focusing questions: 'What is the... like in the group?' What about the...?' 'What are the difficulties with...?' 'How does...?' 'How is...?'

There may be one word answers to some of these questions such as: terrible, pathetic, poor, inefficient, inconsistent etc. Each word, followed by the area named is written on the board as in: inconsistent supply ordering. The facilitator can ask for more concerns about this complaint to be added to the list.

After a while, people might get quite enthusiastic about this process. They may start to shout out things that they've never mentioned before.

It is not uncommon for people to shout out humorous remarks. This is useful because laughter releases tension and there is usually a grain of truth in most humor. The remark is written on the list like everything else. It may need further investigation or it can be discarded later in the process.

Clustering concerns

Some items are probably already grouped together on the list. These and other similar items can now be clustered into common themes. The question could be asked: 'How can some of these items be grouped together?' Or: 'What common thread binds some of these items together?'

These clusters could be written on a Mind Map around a hub expressing the purpose: 'How can we improve', for example. (Mind Maps are described in both our books on meetings.) Each cluster is given a heading such as: Communication. This cluster would include all the things to do with communication within or put out by the group or organization. Other cluster headings could be: management, decision-making, resources, office use, group morale or the reputation of the organization.

This is usually the stage where the basis for many of the concerns begins to emerge. For example: if the organization is seriously under-funded then that is the likely cause of people to feel stressed, overworked, frustrated or ineffective.

> If the leader or the main managers of the project have poor communication skills, this is likely to have a knock-on effect throughout the group.

Ranking

Having got all the gripes and complaints listed and clustered, the participants now rank them in terms of greatest concern. Ranking and prioritizing is not necessarily the same thing. An issue that is ranked as of prime concern may not, for many reasons, be prioritized as the first item to be dealt with.

One of the Ranking processes described in our meeting books could help the participants to identify which they consider to be the most important in descending order.

> Note: There may not be any clear ranking due to the fact that people might experience different things from one another and so have differing concerns. This ought to be seen as interesting information rather than a problem.

Prioritizing

Prioritize each of the ranked clusters in order of being dealt with or in terms of urgency to be addressed. The focusing question for this process will need to take into account what is going on in the organization or group at this time.

Examples:
1. If there is a serious problem with funding or resources, the focusing question might be something like: 'how would we priorities these taking into consideration our financial difficulties?'
2. If there is a critical shortfall in volunteers or volunteers are threatening to leave because of low morale, the question might be: 'what priority shall we give to these considering our volunteer situation? Or 'How shall we prioritize these that will have the most benefit to group moral?'

When the issues have been prioritized the group can then decide when, where and how best to deal with them all.

Next Steps

There are a number of options for these next steps:

Option 1

The rest of the meeting is spent dealing with each of the issues in turn.

Benefits:

Successfully dealing with all the issues in one meeting can give a sense of achievement and a feeling of empowerment in the group. This can allow people to then implement whatever decisions they make about these issues and then get on with their work.

This is a lot to try to achieve in one meeting and will be dependent upon the number of issues identified, the size and seriousness of some of them, the timescale remaining for the meeting and whether or not the people who make decisions (about the budget for example) are present.

Option 2

The meeting is adjourned at this point having scheduled further meetings to deal with each of the issues in order of priority.

Benefits:

People may feel satisfied that the processes undertaken have cleared the air and brought issues out into the open. They may feel complete with this part of the process and eagerly anticipate the future scheduled meetings.

Option 3

The meeting deals with one of the issues raised. This could be the issue that was given priority or one which people feel confident can be fully dealt with in the time remaining. The group then reschedules further meetings to deal with the other issues in order of priority.

Benefits:

If the issue chosen is fully resolved, this can give people a sense of satisfaction and achievement and raise in them an eager anticipation of the future scheduled meetings.

Option 4

The meeting deals with as many as possible of the short, easily manageable items and then schedules further meetings to deal with the larger issues.

Benefits:

Finding workable solutions to a number of niggling items can raise energy levels and create a sense of accomplishment within the group and lead to an excited anticipation of the remaining scheduled meetings.

Option 5

The meeting uses the time remaining to set up working groups, each one with a remit to investigate and consider a different issue. These groups will report back to a whole group meeting on a specified future date. Their suggested options or recommended solutions will be considered and decided upon at that meeting.

Benefits:

This can help people to feel that due care and attention is being paid to their concerns, especially if most, preferably all, the people at the meeting will be engaged in one of these working groups.

Challenges

There are challenges in these options. Some people may not be able to attend future meetings. Not having their concerns addressed immediately might leave some participants feeling incomplete and frustrated. This could compound any belief they have that to attempt changes within the organization is futile. Others might feel concerned that the major issues are being sidestepped or avoided. Indeed, unless these are dealt with in the very near future, they may be right!

Commitment

> If the chosen option means delay in resolving issues, it is vital that any commitments for dealing with them are scrupulously kept to.

Further ongoing meetings are to be scheduled at specific dates and times for the very near future and nothing must happen to prevent them from taking place! Unless these commitments are made and kept the morale and the attitudes within the group or the organization are not likely to improve. In fact, any promises and commitments broken are likely to result in a further decline in morale and effectiveness.

Preventative procedures

Once this process has been completed for the first time, simple procedures for addressing concerns and complaints ought to be created and implemented by the group. Although an Annual Spring Cleaning may still be a good idea, having a system for review for regularly clearing up concerns, complaints and difficulties will prevent a build-up of problems.

This process works well for most types of groups and for almost any project.

6

STARTING PROJECTS

There are two ways to start a project:
1. Just get on and do it.
2. Do some strategic planning.

The first is based on the premises that, if something really needs to be done, just do it, if it generates some objections, you can always apologize afterwards!

It is often easier to get agreement, cooperation and support for something that people can see is working, or has potential, than it is to get permission to begin a project - especially if you have been thinking outside the box and come up with ideas that other people might have difficulty grasping, or in which they might only see limitations or problems.

Once something is up and running it is much easier for people to see the benefits and to consider how they could support and get involved.

Example:
An example of this is the Incredible Edibles project in Todmorden, in the North of England. This was started by a small group of people who wanted places to grow food in their local area for consumption by the local community.

In this town there was very little spare land available for this project and so the group just started planting in whichever spaces seemed appropriate – and some places that might be considered by some to be not appropriate at all!

This project has changed the way this small town looks and eats. Food is now grown all over the place, in every imaginable - and several unimaginable places around the town. People who have never grown anything before have discovered the joy of growing things and realized that they have green fingers. Children now know exactly where their fruit and vegetables come from. The cost of fruit and vegetables has come down and the consumption of healthy food has gone up. In this small town that was founded during the industrial revolution there is greenery everywhere and an abundance of fresh food for the picking.

The founders of that project talk about the organic nature of the development and expansion of their project – perhaps appropriate for a gardening project! They explain that they had an idea and just got on with it. They simply started planting in disused or little used areas of the town. This inspired others to join in and the project seemed to take on a life of its own.

They learned what they needed to learn as they went along and the people with whatever skills became necessary just turned up or were easily coaxed into participating. As the project spread throughout the town, became more complex, and perhaps larger than first envisioned, systems were devised and put into place to manage whatever needed to be managed.

These people enthusiastically extol the virtues of just getting on with making the difference that is desired or necessary and see what happens!

Check the website for a tool-kit, loads of other information and especially for inspiration: http://www.incredible-edible-todmorden.co.uk

This can be an effective way to establish a project for which the need or benefit is obvious, for which there is a lot of enthusiasm, and where nothing similar already exists.

Planning

For most projects however, some strategic planning is useful. For many, it may be essential, especially if a lot of money is involved or there are legal requirements to be met.

For many people, the most exciting aspects of starting a project are the envisioning of its potential, the planning for its development and the creation of systems and structures to support the activities and ongoing sustainability.

> It can be a lot of fun for a group to work together on this. For a new group that has been formed for the purpose of the project this process can deepen relationships, bind the group together and help everyone involved to have a good understanding of the whole picture.

It could also be beneficial to engage with other supportive people who have some necessary specialist skills. Many people would love an opportunity to make a difference to a project that inspires them. Seek them out and invite them to share their knowledge and skills and be part of your exciting venture. An efficient, effective and fun way to engage in some planning and kick start a project is to follow the example set by the inspirational people in the Good for Nothing project:

Good for Nothing!

This is a community of thinkers, doers, makers and tinkerers applying their skills and energy to accelerating the work of cause-led innovators and change makers. It is about diverse groups of people collaborating together, working in new, faster, fun and better ways. It is about working with ideas and people that are leading the way to what a flourishing 21st-century society might look like.

Good for Nothing works in 2 main ways: firstly, through 4 to 48 hour think/hack/do creative, collaboration events; and secondly through web-based missions and an emerging web platform.

Good for Nothing is a growing community of smart folk who collaborate with social innovators, social business and enterprise, activists, change makers, filmmakers and charities. The community welcomes anyone with skills who has a desire to get stuck in.

Those involved give time, money and energy to do stuff that supports people trying to make a positive impact and change. They are doing this through creative, collaborative gigs. These bring together a large diverse group of talented people to work with grassroots, cause-led social innovators in a playful, competitive, experiential experience lasting between 4 and 48 hours.

Good for Nothing is about bringing these people together and seeing what happens. It's also about exploring fun, open, collaborative and self-organized ways of working.

Good for Nothing is founded on 3 core practices:
1. Doing, not talking

It's not hard to talk clever and think big and there's an oversupply of that in our world. Too often big thinking doesn't lead to big doing. We look around and see so much that needs doing. Roll up your sleeves and 'fail gloriously' as Duke Stump once said. Good for Nothing stands for permission to have a go, get involved, participate, and to try stuff.

2. Collaboration and experimentation

Words we all hear a lot, however, true collaboration is where real diversity and openness is welcomed, where we let go of power and control, where we self-organize and allow ideas and energy to emerge more naturally and where we prototype and develop them rapidly. We want to do more of that.

3. Support the true innovators

Give creative energy to the real innovators who are trying to make positive change happen. When we look around for social, environmental and human innovation, a lot of the most exciting stuff is happening at the grass roots. We provide creative support to those pioneers. We think that can help accelerate positive change and impact.

The Rules of the Game at the events are:
Having up to 48 hours to do good for nothing.
Break the rules and see how far you can get.
Be useful. When you aren't; move on. If you can help other teams - do.
There is no expert panel; everyone say's what they love.
This doesn't need to stop tomorrow!

Learning by doing has become a bit of a mantra at the good for nothing base camp. The result has often been hectic, occasionally bonkers but always an incredibly exciting rollercoaster ride for the growing community of good for nothings. See more on the website:
http://www.goodfornothing.com/about/

> By being and doing good for nothing anyone with skills and expertise can help with the startup of local projects.

Advisors

Some specialist information or experience needed for a project's success might not be available within the group membership. Seek advice from elsewhere. Perhaps some people who do not have time to be group members would be prepared to be part of an advisory group.

There is a lot of wisdom and experience going to waste out there. Through voluntary or enforced retirement, redundancy or unemployment there are many people with valuable knowledge, skills and experience who are no longer in a position to use them. These people, especially retirees, may not want to find replacement employment or to spend a lot of their newly acquired leisure time in a working environment. However, they may be willing to spend a small amount of time offering their knowledge and experience in an advisory capacity. This might also apply to people who through promotion or a change of career are no longer using some of their skills and experience.

Experts can advise on almost any subject: fundraising and financial systems; management strategies and service provision; IT systems and communications; people management; meeting methods; handling statutory bodies and the media and many more areas that could be beneficial to organizations, groups and projects.

An advisory panel can provide a project with much of the expertise it requires. This can also do away with the need to set up the management of the project along hierarchical lines in order to have experts involved at a top level. Instead, advisers can support the project to be managed co-operatively within a flatter structure; one in which a greater number of those involved in the project participate in its management and decision-making processes.

Put the word out and ask around. People working in businesses or agencies may know of people within them or former colleagues now retired or moved on who might be willing and interested in voluntarily advising your group.

Using Advisors

Many projects in the Third Sector are instigated and managed by very caring people. These are often the kind of people who don't like to upset others, who try to make everything nice for everyone, who want to work in a relaxed, harmonious, companionable and cooperative environment and who prefer to avoid making tough decisions, especially if these are likely to be unpopular with some people.

Whilst these attitudes have many advantages, both for the people working in the organization and for the people receiving care and support from it, they can also create problems. They can lead to inefficiency, ineffectiveness, frustration and possibly non-sustainability.

Advice offered on how to do things differently within an organization to alleviate some of these problems is obviously likely to include developing attitudes, making decisions and taking actions that are opposite to the ones that have created the current problems. This can create resistance by people in the project to acting upon the advice given by people from outside the group - regardless of how professional or experienced these people may be.

This could be because some people within the project feel embarrassed at having their faults or failures identified. Some might feel reluctant to implement procedures and processes with which they are unfamiliar or that they consider to be alien to the project or perhaps their culture.

> As even inefficient or ineffective people will have probably been doing the very best they could do, it would be sensible – and kind - to acknowledge and appreciate their efforts and to introduce the advised new or revised procedures to them in a manner they would find easily acceptable.

Making the most of advisors
- Be clear about what kind of advice you need.
- Become aware of what kind of advice is on offer.
- Provide your advisers with all the information they need upon which to base their advice.
- Have advisers liaise with the appropriate people in your group/organization/project.
- Have everyone or representatives of everyone who will be affected by any advised changes present at their presentations.
- Create opportunities for those people to have discussions and to offer ideas and suggestions for how these advised changes could be best implemented.

Be open-minded
Not all advice will be applicable and some might not be very palatable.

> However, there is no point in seeking advice if you do not intend to follow at least some of that advice.

I have observed a number of occasions where organizations have sought advice from experts and then rejected that advice because it did not fit the culture of that organization. 'We don't do that sort of thing', 'that's not who we are', 'that won't work here', are phrases that I heard expressed to well-intentioned people offering advice based upon years of experience.

Rejecting or accepting advice
Rejecting

> It will be wise to resist any temptation to reject advice out of hand.

Refusing to consider making the advised changes will probably result in business as usual, which might not only result in your problems remaining, it could also gain you a reputation for inflexibility and unwillingness to be advised.

You also have some responsibility towards the person whose advice you have sought. I have witnessed well-intentioned experts feeling disrespected when the advice they carefully gave was ignored or rejected. As a result of this, other experts were not so willing to offer advice in the future.

If, for whatever reason, the advice sought is not going to be taken then this ought to be communicated respectfully to the advisor. He or she deserves a full explanation of the reasons for rejecting their advice and ought to be appropriately appreciated for their efforts to be supportive and for the precious time they have given.

Accepting

Implementing advised changes might be difficult for some people in the organization and could lead them to feel disappointed or frustrated in being unable to continue to work in their preferred manner. They may feel that their well-meaning approaches to working have not been successful, appreciated, valued or properly understood.

Implementing advice to radically change attitudes and working practices might result in discontentment or resentment within the organization - especially if the people affected do not understand why those changes are necessary.

Finding a middle way

In my experience there is usually a middle way to be found in most situations. Even if the adviser does not understand the culture of your organization or the reasons behind the development of that culture they are still likely to have offered some suggestions that could sensibly be taken.

Options:
a. Advice sought from experts ought to be carefully considered.
b. Look for bits of the advice that could be taken.
c. Implement any advised changes in small incremental steps whenever possible.
d. Bring everyone involved on board in making these changes.
e. Explain what these changes are, why they are necessary and what they are intended to achieve.
f. Seek ideas and suggestions from those to be affected by the changes on how these would be best implemented.
g. Monitor progress and have simple feedback systems in place.
h. Keep your advisors updated with the progress and results of their

advice.

Individuals and organizations rarely seek advice when things are going well. Advice is usually sought only when things are going badly or when people don't know what they can do to improve some situation or to prevent some potential calamity. This might be described as 'fire-fighting'.

Remember: To prevent the 'fires' from starting it could be a good strategy to do the assessment of needs and requesting of advice in periods of calm.

Strategies for success

It is possible that small, simple projects that are developed and managed by a handful of people may not appear to need much in the way of strategies in order to be effective. Sometimes it is necessary to just get on and do things.

> Even so, in most cases it is my experience that having strategies right from the start for the various functions and stages of a project is better than not.

In starting up a project the strategies would include:
- Clarifying the purpose and objectives.
- Identifying the need for the project.
- Setting up the most appropriate legal and management structures.

In developing the project culture the strategies would involve:
- Establishing ethics and values.
- Making group agreements.
- Creating procedures for maintaining cooperation, dealing with conflict, managing meetings and making decisions.

For achieving the desired outcomes the strategies would include:
- Identifying those to receive benefit from the project.
- Creating the processes and procedures for delivering those objectives and benefits.
- Identifying the means for acquiring the necessary resources – funding, equipment, services and advisers.

Maintaining effectiveness and relevance the strategies would include:
- Methods for monitoring activities, measuring and evaluating results.
- Means for reporting on progress.
- Procedures for feedback.
- Ways of estimating continued relevance.

Q

Important questions to consider

Before initiating any project it would be wise to carefully consider the following questions:

A. What is the purpose of the project?
B. What is the reason for initiating this project?
C. Is there any real need for it?
D. Who is already attempting to deal with this need?
E. How well are they doing?
F. Would it be more appropriate to be part of what they are doing?
G. Could your proposed project or group work co-operatively with what already exists?

A. Clearly stating your objectives will help you and other people to understand what to expect from your project and what you and they can offer to it. A section is devoted to this a little later in the book after some consideration is given to the reasons for initiating the project and some research into the need for it.

B. What is the reason for initiating this project?

Being clear about the reasons for creating a project can save a lot of time and effort and can make it obvious what strategies will needed. These reasons might be important to the initiator yet not so to other people. If the reasons are very personal to the initiator, the project might not attract the support it needs. On the other hand, a person with a great deal of passion for a project even if it will only benefit them or someone they care about, can inspire support from many other people.

C. Is there a genuine need for it?

In my experience, having established some idea of what the project is intended to achieve and the reasons for its initiation, it is vital to ensure that there is a real need for it.

There are many similarities in starting a project to that of starting a business. The failure of some businesses occurs when the enthusiasm of the proprietors is greater than the real need for their product or service. This also applies to voluntary or community projects.

The first essential step is to do some research into the viability of the project by assessing the need and estimating the competition.

It is surprising how frequently projects are initiated to fulfill some purpose that has not been properly thought through, upon which hardly any research has been done, for which there is little recognizable need or where such need is already being catered for.

I have observed that sometimes this is because people get a bee in their bonnet about an issue based on their own experience or that of someone they care about. This emotional reaction might galvanize people into action before sufficient thought, research and evaluation has taken place.

There are many real needs to be catered for. Perhaps a service that is not currently being provided; some problems that require remedial action, or a growing desire amongst citizens for ways to become involved in making improvements in their community. However, there is an important supplementary question to first consider:

Whose need is it?

During consultations with people intending to create projects or groups I have become aware that occasionally the desire of some individuals to initiate a project can be more about their own needs than any real requirement for such a project to exist.

Such a need might be for some kind of support or service that would specifically benefit their own situation or perhaps that of a relatively few people.

It could be sensible to carry out an assessment of the real size of the need. If choosing to continue with the initiative, it might be wise to scale the operation to fit the size of the actual need. I have seen situations where the setting up of a project that was larger than was necessary proved to be an unsustainable use of time, effort and resources.

A person's need might be to become the initiator and manager of a project or the leader of a group. In which case, the stated purpose of the project is likely to be of secondary importance to them than their role within it. Although, in these circumstances, a project may still be worthwhile supporting - people attracted to such a project would be wise to keep this in mind.

Establishing the need

One method of establishing if there is a need for your project is to conduct a survey. Surveys and questionnaires could become part of listening to the people within your community, especially those whom your project is intended to serve. This might require a widely conducted survey or involve one-to-one interviews with key people or stakeholder leaders or representatives to identify needs and concerns and to discover what is already being done. The results of these will inform your strategies and activities

Some suggestions for designing a survey questionnaire:
- Be clear about what it is that you want to know, the reasons for the survey and what you want to learn from it.
- Be inclusive in your sample survey in order to get as representative a spread of appropriate people as possible across the board.
- Make the questionnaire short and concise because most people are busy and are unlikely to be happy to answer endless questions.
- Use simple, plain and accessible language. Avoid jargon and complex or lengthy questions.
- Avoid asking leading questions.
- For the integrity of the survey to be fully respected keep the tone as impartial and unbiased as possible.
- Try a questionnaire out on a few people first to iron out any oddities, any questions that are confusing or which don't make sense.

There is skill in designing an effective questionnaire and just as much in collating and understanding the collected data. This might be an occasion to bring in someone with this skill and knowledge around statistics. This might be a role for one of your advisors or someone wanting to gain experience in this field.

The first community survey that I commissioned was written, conducted and processed by a final year student looking for field experience. She did a brilliant job; we received vital information and she gained the experience she needed for her dissertation. Win-Win!

Other research

It could be wise to also gather information about people's opinions, attitudes and expectations. You could conduct interviews to explore through a series of open questions what those involved in such a project would perceive as being successful. You might also organize some focus groups for brainstorming what people would consider to be indicators that a project had been a success or not. You will then have these to measure against throughout the project and at its conclusion.

D. Who is already attempting to deal with this need?

This is important to recognize. Any attempt to initiate a project in an area that is already well served by other projects could limit the effectiveness of your project. It might also divert much-needed resources from the established projects. By creating unnecessary competition for limited resources you might be creating more problems than solutions.

E. How well are they doing?

It might be vital to your success to check out how well an existing project is doing. You may discover that they are successfully achieving what you would hope to do. In which case starting another project may undermine their success and limit the possibilities of your own.

If it seems they are not doing very well it would be wise to investigate the reasons for that. You might discover that the reasons are outside their control. Lack of any real interest or support, restrictive regulations, or other difficulties and obstacles that are limiting their success could very well limit yours.

F. Could you be a part what they are doing?

Could your proposed project or group become a useful part of a project that already exists? You might not need to create another project if your group's skills and enthusiasm could be offered and accepted by an existing similar project.

G. Could you work cooperatively with another project?

Could your proposed project or group work co-operatively with, alongside and in support of a project that already exists? If an existing project is successfully doing what you want to do could you add to their success by contributing your own skills and experience? If the people in an existing project are not managing to achieve what you want to achieve is it possible that they might be able to do so if they had the benefit of your experience, skills and support?

> If the benefits of a project are not obvious – or are only so to one person, if there is currently little enthusiasm for such a project, and, if other similar projects are already in existence locally, it would be sensible to give some careful thought and consideration to the wisdom of launching a project.

If, after doing all of this research, you are convinced that your project is needed and has every chance of being successful then get started on planning your strategies; letting your intentions be known and attracting the support that you need.

If the group to support the project hasn't yet been formed, this would be the time to do that.

Statement of purpose and objectives

> This ought to be a statement that clearly shows the intended purpose of the project.

This might be part of the articles of Association of a group. It could form the strap-line under the name of a project or an organization or it could be referred to in the Mission Statement. Whatever this statement is called, ideally, it ought to be succinct and easily remembered.

Sometimes the statement of objectives is the same as the statement of purpose and sometimes it needs to be created separately and in more detail.

> Creating a clear statement of the objectives of the project ought to be done with all of those involved. People feel far more committed to something that they have had a hand in creating; so finding the words that encapsulate the essence of the objectives of the project would best be done through a group process.

Words have power

Words are remarkably powerful. They have the power to persuade, to encourage, to include and to inspire people. They also have the power to alienate. It would be wise to carefully choose the words of your statement.

The group processes chosen to produce this statement ought to include opportunities for thinking out loud, for being creative and expansive and then refining and defining ideas. Brainstorming and Refining and any other process that allow everyone to have a say would be helpful. Many of these can be found in the books: ENJOYABLE & EFFECTIVE MEETINGS and EFFORTLESS FACILITATION in this series, available form Amazon and accessible through: www.youmakethedifference.net/books

Additional Objectives

Although there is usually one obvious objective, there may be some additional aims that could be very important. Such as the attitudes within the group, in what spirit the work will be done and what else might be achieved along the way. To bring everyone on board it may be helpful to go through a refining process in which the essence of all these aims can be distilled and included.

The following are some examples of succinct yet encompassing statements:

First Principle of the John Lewis Partnership:
The Partnership's ultimate purpose is the happiness of all its members, through their worthwhile and satisfying employment in a successful business.

Oxfam International's mission statement:
Oxfam International is an international group of independent non-governmental organizations dedicated to fighting poverty and related injustice around the world. The Oxfams work together internationally to achieve greater impact by their collective efforts.

And even:
Star Trek - 5-Year Mission:
To explore strange new worlds, to seek out new life and new civilizations, to boldly go where no one has gone before!

> Statements of purpose and of aims and objectives can sometimes be so lengthy and involved that they lose their punch.

Instead of being clear and concise these statements can be muddled and complex. Rather than engaging people such statements might lose their interest. The common cause of this is usually an attempt to come up with a statement that pleases all the people involved. This can be difficult to achieve when the membership of a group includes people with predominantly differing ways of receiving and processing information and for whom different words have special meaning and power.

Visual, Auditory and Kinesthetic people

Although we each use most of our senses to learn - to recognize, receive, process and retain information - most of us have one mode: Visual, Auditory or Kinesthetic, that is predominant.

Visual people

These people prefer to receive their information visually. They like to see things and often think in pictures. Symbols have power for them and they can take in a lot of information from a picture or a graphic image. These people are often visually creative. They usually have an eye for good design and have good color sense. When expressing ideas, a predominantly visual person may often use expressions such as: 'I see... It looks as if... I noticed that...' Their speech will be peppered with visually descriptive words.

Auditory people

These people prefer to receive their information through words and sounds. They learn best through reading and listening and can usually remember much of what they hear and read. Predominantly auditory people are often musical and creative with the written word. When expressing ideas, a predominantly auditory person might use expressions such as: 'I hear that... It sounds as though...' Their speech will contain auditory descriptive words.

Kinesthetic people

These people mostly receive their information through experiences and feelings. They like to learn through experiencing and doing. Predominantly kinesthetic people are often attracted to professions and pastimes where they can express their feelings or demonstrate care. They might be involved in dance, some types of theatre and tactile forms of self-expression; body work such as massage, and supportive activities like counseling. When expressing ideas, predominantly kinesthetic people might use expressions such as: 'I feel that... I have a sense that...' The words they use can be heavily biased towards those of feelings.

Make a note

It could be interesting for you to make a note of the way you best receive your information to consider which of these modalities is your prominent one.

Putting it all together

When creating a statement of objectives, predominantly visual people are likely to want it to conjure up a visual image in the mind; auditory folk may prefer detailed written information and those with strong kinesthetic tendencies might desire the statement to evoke emotion.

Too much emphasis on any one of these modalities can turn off people with other predominant modes. For example, projects in the fields of spirituality, healing or some aspects of personal growth can attract a high proportion of kinesthetic people. However, statements of objectives that have been put out by some of these groups have been considered by non-kinesthetic people to be at best 'warm and fuzzy'; at worst, too 'flaky' to be taken seriously.

> Creating a concise statement using some elements from each of the Visual, Auditory and Kinesthetic language modes is likely to have the most impact upon the greatest number of people.

Commitment to excellence

When the people involved in a project are choosing to do so, there is likely to be a strong commitment to achieving excellence in all aspects of it.

A wise strategy for achieving this is to put in place systems for recording and monitoring progress and measuring and evaluating results.

I believe that Voluntary and Community Projects deserve the same commitment to the levels of excellence as might be found in organizations that provide products and services for which they are well paid. In this commitment to excellence it ought to make no difference whether the people working in these projects are paid staff or volunteers. The receivers of this voluntary work have a right for that to be offered in a professional and caring manner.

However, in voluntary projects the motivation for this commitment may be different in the paid staff and the volunteers. Even though both these groups of people may have their heart in the project, it could be wise to be aware that there are usually more direct and obvious benefits for the paid staff than for the volunteers. Having said that, I have observed that the passion for a project can sometimes be greater in the volunteers than in the paid employees.

Volunteering

Volunteer does not mean amateur

> It is vital for volunteers in a project to take their responsibilities seriously.

Even though volunteers are not being paid for the work they carry out, that does not diminish the importance of that work. It does not mean that they can turn up late when volunteering or be over casual, careless or slipshod when they get there. People will be relying upon them to do what they are required to do when they are needed to do it.

Unfortunately, some professionals and paid workers in some organizations and in public sector departments still look down on volunteers who they often consider to be amateur. Fortunately there are now positive signs that this view is changing.

It is worth remembering that many volunteers hold or have held positions of rank and responsibility in their professional and private lives. Some volunteers may very well be more qualified, skilled and experienced than some employed people. However, a casual approach to their work by any volunteer could damage the reputation for professionalism that so many people have worked hard to establish in the Voluntary and Community Sector.

> Volunteers can help maintain this reputation and make the difference by helping to change any outdated attitudes regarding the amateurism of volunteers by being as professional as possible in all volunteering activities.

Volunteering is not about sacrifice or being a martyr.

There are some jobs that are uncomfortable, unpleasant or uninteresting that need to be done by somebody. Those do not always have to be the same people. Even though difficult or tiresome jobs can be humbling and that can be useful for keeping the ego in check, I would have some concern about a person who consistently volunteers for unpleasant, extremely challenging or tedious work, when there are others who could take their turn with these tasks. I have observed that when these types of jobs are rotated within the project this can offer many people the opportunity to develop humility and perhaps compassion for those less fortunate than themselves.

The book ENJOYABLE & VALUABLE VOLUNTEERING suggests ways for people to achieve and maintain high levels of excellence in their volunteering. There are also methods for supporting volunteers to reach high standards of excellence in the book EMPOWERING VOLUNTEER MANAGEMENT. These are available in paperback and e-book versions from Amazon and are accessible through our website: www.youmakeethedifference.net/books

7

LEGAL AND MANAGEMENT STRUCTURES

There are many organizational legal structures to choose from. These include: Unincorporated Associations, Trusts, Limited Companies, Social Enterprises, Charitable Incorporated Organizations, Co-operatives, Industrial and Provident Societies, Community Benefit Societies and Community Interest Companies.

Even though the following Link is to the UK Government Business Link site, it offers a great deal of information that could be useful to the Third Sector in the UK as well as to people in other countries. It covers information on the various structures mentioned above.

www.businesslink.gov.uk/bdotg/action/layer?topicId=1077475650

Until relatively recently, the most common forms of Voluntary and Community groups and organizations have been Trusts, Charitable Organizations Limited by Guarantee or, for small groups, Unincorporated Associations. Through innovative thinking over the last couple of decades new structures have been devised that allow for a more modern approach to fulfilling the needs within communities. A model that is gaining in popularity is that of Social Enterprise, which is suitable for organizations that are able to generate some of their own income.

Social Enterprise

The main benefit in developing a Social Enterprise is the greater autonomy it provides to a project. In being able to create income a Social Enterprise is less dependent upon traditional forms of fundraising.

It seems to me that in the foreseeable future, Grants are going to be harder to find and available funding from traditional sources is going to be sought after by increasing numbers of potentially desperate organizations.

> Being able to generate some income allows a Social Enterprise to be self-determining to some extent and to utilize supportive and ethical business models.

Some enterprises have goods to sell, the profits from which support social activities or provide some benefit to others. Other enterprises offer services, sometimes, essential services, for which they can be remunerated.

Whatever form a Social Enterprise takes, it is imperative that the intention is to be of **social benefit**. This is what distinguishes a Social Enterprise from a business that is run to create profit for its owners, shareholders or investors.

The following description of Social Enterprise is from the UK Government website mentioned above:

A Social Enterprise is a business with primarily social objectives whose surpluses are principally reinvested for that purpose in the business or in the community, rather than being driven by the need to maximize profit for shareholders and owners.

Within this definition, Social Enterprises can take on a variety of legal forms, including:
Unincorporated Associations
Trusts
Limited Companies
Some Industrial and Provident Societies such as Community Benefit Societies
Community Interest Companies
Charitable Incorporated Organizations.

A Social Enterprise should also consider whether or not to set itself up as a charity. Doing so offers a number of benefits, including significant tax reliefs, but results in increased regulation and less flexibility.

It is what a business does with its profits that determines whether it is a Social Enterprise, rather than its specific legal structure. However, you should carefully consider the various options to ensure that you choose the legal structure that most suits your social enterprise in terms of management style and mission. Although professional advice is not always necessary, it is a good idea to seek the opinion of an expert before coming to a decision.

Not–for–profit distribution

There are many people who are skeptical of the idea of Social Enterprise. For them, the words enterprise and social do not sit comfortably together because they believe there is no place for enterprise in any form of not–for–profit venture. The shift to the concept of '**not–for–profit distribution**' could alleviate these concerns. This of course does require that any profits generated by a Social Enterprise are always reinvested in the enterprise or are used for social or community benefit and are not paid out to shareholders or investors.

In a climate where investors are looking for new areas of financial return on investment, Social Enterprises seem to offer interesting potential, particularly to people who would like to see their money making some positive social or environmental difference. However, care needs to be taken both by the investors and the Social Enterprises who are considering these possibilities. A very small percentage of Social Enterprises make sufficient profit to give much, if any, of a return on investment. The requirement, expectation or demand from investors in a Social Enterprise might oblige that organization to reduce its social commitment in order to fulfill those expectations of financial return.

An obvious way for Social Enterprises to differentiate themselves from businesses is for them to create, proclaim, and adhere to a clear code of practice, which states the values, ethics, and behaviors that identify them, preferably one set as a national standard. Below is the inspirational Voluntary Code of Practice created by and for Social Enterprises in Scotland in 2012.

Voluntary code of practice for Social Enterprise

(Created by Social Enterprise Scotland)

Context

In 2002, the UK Government published an 'official' definition of social enterprise (SE) which was also adopted in Scotland. The ensuing 10 years has seen a dramatic rise in the popularity of SE; a tide which no-one could have anticipated and shows no sign of turning. But the government definition was never invested with sufficient authority to be effective. In England, in particular, there has been a lobby to keep definitions blurred; with the result that essentially private businesses are masquerading as SEs and devaluing the brand.

In response to this drift, the Scottish SE community has set down the values and behaviours by which we recognize each other. We refer to this document as a voluntary code of practice – or simply the Code. Whereas a mandatory set of rules runs the risk of inviting dispute and division – it is hoped that this voluntary code can provide the basis for a self-regulating community. By setting this 'benchmark', we clarify our shared vision and distinguish it from other approaches.

The Code distinguishes between the Basics and Values/Behaviours.

1. The Basics

This section details the essential elements of a social enterprise (SE). It would be exceptional for any business that does not meet these criteria to be considered a SE.

i. SEs are businesses operating in markets – usually selling goods and services – whose primary objective is to achieve social and environmental benefit.
ii. Regardless of its legal form, the constitution of a SE will include the requirement that profits are reinvested in the business or in the beneficiary community – and not distributed to owners/shareholders/investors. *See below.
iii. The constitution will always require that on dissolution, the assets of the SE are redirected appropriately – this could include to SEs with similar aims and objectives.
iv. Taken together these two provisions are referred to as the 'asset lock' - which is the defining characteristic of a SE.
v. SEs are distinguished from the private sector by virtue of the asset lock.
vi. SEs are differentiated from those charities and voluntary organizations in the third sector that do not aspire to financial independence through trading.
vii. SEs are distinct from the public sector and cannot be the subsidiary of a public body.

* This Code does not exclude that certain types of social enterprise could be 'honourable exemptions' to the zero dividend norm. But this number is very small.

2. Values/Behaviors

SE is a relatively recent term but it comes out of values developed throughout the history of our social economy. Its core principle is that economic activity should work for the common good – rather than the unlimited private gain of a few. This locates SE within the wider objective of changing the way society operates. Various social movements have contributed their DNA to SE practice. These are some of the Values/Behaviours we have come to expect from each other.

Values:

SEs are businesses founded on fundamental core values – that social fairness and the protection of the planet should be pre-conditions of all economic activity – with all business practices expected to be honest and fair.

Good employers:
SEs are good employers – trying to offer a good workplace experience; aiming to pay a 'living wage'; and having flatter pay structures than the private sector. A maximum ratio of 1:5 between lowest and highest is a useful guide.

Democratic:
From Co-ops and Mutual's, SEs have learned about common ownership and democratic governance.

Empowerment:
From Development Trusts and the community business movement, SEs have learned about bottom up responses to social problems and how they empower local communities.

Collaboration:
Within the common sense of running a business – SEs try to help and support one another - in the spirit of the Open Source IT community. SEs should also, where possible, encourage the practice of intra-trading i.e. procuring from within the sector itself.

3. Our Operating Landscape

Based on shared values and the desire to build their businesses – SEs are increasingly finding ways to collaborate. The growth of the Scottish SE community, into a fully blown 'movement' - capable of 'changing the way society operates' - depends on a favourable operating landscape. Aspects of our landscape will depend on the support of Government at all levels - European, UK, Scottish, local authorities. But it is our community itself which best understands what is needed. These are some of the lessons of the past decade.

Bespoke Support:
SEs need business support structures embedded in the culture of our own community. Such support should be accessible to all – from start-ups through to national contractors.

Bespoke investment:
It is not appropriate for SEs to strive to be investment vehicles in the normal sense; we need investment from sources that support social aims and our own 'mutual' investment funds – based on SE values.

Sustainable procurement:
Our landscape should reflect the potential for the growth of SE into the area of public contracts – that are weighted towards social and environmental benefits, including community benefit clauses.

Unity:
Vibrant communities like ours, accommodate and are strengthened by a wide range of disparate views – and yet speak with a united voice.

SE Networks:
So that relationships can be built, and reciprocal help flourish – frontline Networks should be encouraged in all areas that want one – and be independent and self-sufficient.

Author's note: This seems to me to be a carefully thought out Voluntary Code of Practice that Social Enterprise in many other countries could beneficially use as a template.

Transition Enterprise

These are a variation on Social Enterprises that have evolved out of the Transition Town Movement. Along with community sustainability they usually operate with a high level of environmental awareness. In researching this topic I found the following description from the Transition Town website.

Characteristics of a Transition Enterprise

1. Resilience outcome – *TEs contribute to the increased resilience of communities in the face of, for example, economic uncertainty, energy and resource shortages and climate change impacts. As part of their community, TEs are also resilient in themselves, seeking to be financially sustainable and as independent as possible of external funding.*

2. Appropriate resource use - *TEs make efficient and appropriate use of natural resources (including energy), respecting finite limits and minimizing and integrating waste streams. The use of fossil fuels in particular is minimized.*

3. Appropriate localization – *TEs operate at a scale appropriate to the environment, economy and business sector with regard to sourcing, distribution and interaction with the wider economy.*

4. More than profit – *TEs exist to provide affordable, sustainable products and services and decent livelihoods rather than to generate profits for others. TEs can be profitable, but the use of their excess profits prioritizes the community benefit rather than benefit to investors.*

5. Part of the community - *TEs work towards building a common wealth, owned and controlled as much as is practical by their workers, customers, users, tenants and communities. They have structures or business models, which are as open, autonomous, equitable, democratic, inclusive and accountable as possible. They complement and work in harmony with other TEs.*

See more: http://www.transitionnetwork.org/about.

This website also offers very useful information on many topics of interest to community groups and projects. Here is what is available on the subject of legal entities and insurance:

Legal entities

Many people switch off in conversations about legal structures. Yet the legal structure of a group affects its behavior and how it is seen by others. Flexibility and informality is fine for a young initiative, but as you grow and take on more responsibilities you will need more structure and allocation of responsibility.

No single approach fits every Transition group. You have to decide what is right for you, depending on what you are doing or planning, what sources of funding you intend to apply to and how well the group can handle administration such as minute keeping and filing returns. You also need to consider how more formality will affect the group (for example, some people are unfamiliar with and suspicious of formal structures and may feel excluded by too formal an approach).

You may eventually need more than one entity. If you decide to set up a business, for example, you will have to create an independent organization (probably a Community Interest Company or a cooperative to own it). The structure does not have to be permanent – you can change your legal form to match your circumstances. Doing so is time consuming and can be expensive, but there is no need to be trapped in an unsuitable structure.

You must decide whether to apply to register as a charity. The aims of most Transition groups will qualify as charitable. Registering as a charity makes fundraising easier. However, the registration process is slow and can be tricky for those unfamiliar with the procedures. Once established, you must make sure you comply with charity law and the rules set out by the Charity Commission.

For many groups, the right initial choice will be to form a club (or 'unincorporated association', to give it its full legal name). This is easy to set up (a simple constitution must be drawn up and signed) and has minimal ongoing formality or administration. Provided the club's income is less than £1,000 per year, you don't have to register as a charity. Clubs need a written constitution that is formally adopted by the group.

Sample constitutions of Transition groups

These can be found online, and you can copy one and adapt it for your needs. Some groups may be happy to remain a club; others may decide to become a limited company –

a step up in complexity and administration. This should be quite straightforward – conversion from a club to a company is hardly more complicated than forming a new company.

You should view choosing and forming a legal structure as an opportunity to clarify the group's vision and aims. The legal structure should not be chosen by a small clique and imposed on the group. It is far better to arrange for proper discussion about the options, to allow the parts of your group to have their say.

The legal structure can support your relationships with third parties. For example, you might invite the local council to be a 'member' of your legal entity (whether a club or a company). This lets them vote on many key decisions made by the group (including appointment of the committee or board) and will give them proper involvement. A more informal way of linking with your collaborators would be to invite individuals employed by the partner to become members of your group. This makes the committee more accountable and reduces the risk of a clique dominating the group and excluding others.

Choosing the right legal structure for your group doesn't need to be dull. The process can help clarify what the group is about and how it can organize itself. Learn from others who have been through the process. Keep formality to the minimum level possible. For many, a club may be the right form, and this can be set up with a minimum of effort. If you decide to set up a limited company, you may be able to get a grant. The key to long-term success, whatever structure you set up, is to retain flexibility and to ensure that those leading the group are accountable to its members and the community.

Insurance

Another aspect of becoming a formal organization is the area of insurance. There are various types of insurance you will need to take out to protect your group. The following is a brief overview of the types of cover you could take out, with the order of importance from top to bottom.

Employers' Liability

This will cover your group against accidents at work, to both staff and volunteers, for which you are legally liable. This is a statutory requirement, and a certificate of Employers' Liability insurance must be displayed at your main residence. Your insurers will need to know what your annual wage roll is for paid staff and how many volunteers you have working on your Transition initiatives. You are liable as an employer whether or not someone working for you is paid or not. Depending on the activities your group is involved in, it may be prudent to check the credentials of your volunteers with regard to undertaking activities with a general degree of risk – if any.

Public Liability

This protects your group against third-party property damage and/or bodily injury during everyday activities anywhere in the UK. Though not a statutory requirement, it would be extremely inadvisable not to take out this insurance. Both this and Employers' Liability insurance should be viewed as essential.

Professional Indemnity

Protecting your group from advice given to third parties that causes property damage and/or bodily injury or financial loss.

Personal Accident

Cover for injury to volunteers and staff that does not follow from legal liability (Employers' Liability) insurance.

Renewable energy assets

In taking advantage of the Feed-in Tariffs on solar PV or other small renewable energy systems, your group will need to insure the public liability risk and against the potential material damage emanating from its operation. Cover can additionally be obtained for loss of revenue and mechanical breakdown too.

Other assets

Cover for office contents, computers, sheds, exhibition equipment, etc.

Machinery, plant and tools

Cover for any of these used by your group to carry out everyday Transition initiative business.

At the initial stage you will likely need only Employers' Liability and Public Liability insurance, but over time, as your initiative grows, you will need to add to this. Ask your preferred insurance provider to assist you with these.

A comprehensive search on the web will provide more useful information on these topics.

Management structures

In deciding upon a management structure there are a variety from which to choose. Even so, although there is a recognition that within the world of business the managerial structures are flattening out, many groups and organizations in the Third Sector are still usually set up with hierarchical structures of a Board of Trustees, a board of Directors or a management committee. This means that a handful of people, either self-appointed or elected by a membership, have a large measure of or even total control over most of the decisions made.

Many of the people in these positions are wise, altruistic and take their responsibilities seriously. Unfortunately, sometimes, the people in these positions have personal agendas. Some carry out their duties either less than effectively or without due care and attention to how their decisions affect others involved within the organization.

The pitfalls of this type of hierarchical structure are often exacerbated by the mix of volunteers and paid employees within an organization. Employees and volunteers can have different requirements and reasons for their involvement. They might also have different criteria for making decisions and have different ways of measuring success.

My previous book, EMPOWERING VOLUNTEER MANAGEMENT, explores how volunteers in groups and organizations can and ought to be supported by those in managerial positions. The other side of the same coin is how voluntary committees, boards of trustees or directors can best support paid employees.

I have observed and experienced occasions when voluntary boards or committees have made decisions that have not taken into account the advice from, or the wellbeing of, paid employees. Also, times when necessary actions have not been taken by them to guarantee those employees the resources or support they have needed to carry out their work.

The letter below is one person's experience of this. Written out of frustration and disappointment, this letter highlights the difficulties that can be experienced by employees who are managed by voluntary boards or committees. When these boards do not include employees in any of the decision-making and whose actions, or lack of, put the security of people's employment, and sometimes the organization, at risk.

To provide confidentiality the frequent references to 'the organization' have replaced that organization's name.

Letter:

Some of you will know that I no longer work for the organization although you may not be unaware of the true reasons why I left.

I believe serious governance issues forced my resignation, caused three people to lose their jobs and have put the organization at risk. I hold the board of trustees substantially responsible for this.

Therefore I am writing to those who either work in or work with the third sector to explain the reasons for my sudden departure in the hope some of my experiences might not be repeated. The following comes out of <u>my</u> day-to-day experience of working in this organization and elsewhere.

This letter is not intended to bore you with my personal issues, but about the wider issues of a culture and a system of governance that does not serve the third sector well and ultimately undermines staff well being. Although I do hold the board of trustees responsible for my loss of livelihood, the personal detail of why I felt I was forced to leave is best left for an Industrial Tribunal.

During my time with the organization I along with others made considerable efforts to develop it so that it could continue to deliver meaningful and much needed work in the area. I made considerable personal sacrifices for this aim because I believed there was a huge need for the work we were doing and in the potential for the organization's development. To this end I worked for a lot of the time unpaid. It is also fair to say that I was one of several who worked hard.

However, after almost 2 years I came to the clear view that the organization's small board simply did not have the capacity or structures in place to evolve in tandem with the organization to support its wider development and to exercise a duty of care towards me as General Manager. I was not alone in thinking this within the organization.

Corporate structure

I believe that the legal structure preferred by most third sector organizations and certainly preferred by this one – the private limited company – is totally unsuited to the professed purpose and ethos of most charities. It is a structure imported from the corporate world that is unchanged since Victorian days. To my mind it is like many long established structures in today's world that are no longer fit for purpose. The third sector so often boasts that it is different from the corporate world and yet it uses mostly corporate structures to manage its business.

In my experience this corporate straight jacket creates a mind-set and a hierarchical approach that is not healthy. There is created a division between paid staff - whose livelihoods depend on the organization - and a volunteer board who have great authority over the organization, but whose livelihoods do not depend on the organization and whose individual actions are well protected by limited liability.

This privileged and protected position that board members enjoy can create in my experience an arrogance and a belief in their own infallibility as board members. It's an old fashioned belief that those in authority – in this case the board - cannot ever be wrong. I experienced this first hand within this organization.

I do not believe that being a board member makes a good person bad. We can all be board members at one time or another. It doesn't change who we are. It is the system that we work within that changes our behavior. It is the system I am critical of here.

In my time working and volunteering in the third sector I have both served on boards and reported to boards. I have also helped create voluntary organizations. Without doubt it is challenging to be a board member of an ambitious organization, but on balance it is not your livelihood that is at stake.

In my opinion it is never an equal partnership between paid staff and voluntary boards. Yet the third sector claims to be all about partnership and equality and bizarrely works under these Victorian systems of hierarchical governance.

I know there will be many who will argue that a voluntary board brings objectivity, wider expertise and that people who give up their time to volunteer on boards should be greatly appreciated and not criticized. To me this smacks of the Victorian attitudes that created these legal structures i.e. the great and the good must oversee the activities of others because they know better and they (the great and the good) should not be held to account by lesser beings.

A pool of wider expertise on a board is a great advantage. However an advisory panel rather than a board of trustees can easily provide this

The new structures that have been developed in recent times such as Charitable Incorporated Organizations and Community Interest Companies have improved things somewhat in that they allow staff to be board members. However the most suitable vehicle for the third sector – the Cooperative (although also Victorian in origin) – is, bizarrely, the least used. I have come to conclude that this is because the third sector is most comfortable with hierarchical, corporate structures.

When I recently proposed some staff membership of this organization's board it was resisted. It became clear to me that this was because such a change was seen as an unwelcome change to the status quo and a potential threat to the board's much valued authority. I was left reflecting why these good people felt like this.

Governance

Unfortunately, while many voluntary board members are individually highly motivated, experienced and ethical, many see board membership as furthering their social or career status. Too many boards are self-appointing – like this organization - and too few board members have a clear appreciation of what an organization needs and what they can personally offer. Moreover, boards must recognize that their individual expertise is one thing, but it is how they perform and act collectively that is so vital to their organization. How many boards are skilled at good collective and collaborative working?

In all issues of management I believe there must be an equal balance between responsibility and authority. Too often in poorly governed organization's staff have all the responsibility but no authority, while the board has all the authority but no responsibility or as in this case it fluctuated back and forth and we never worked out where the balance lay: confusion resulted about management roles leading in the end to ill feeling. As ever, <u>staff paid the price in the loss of employment.</u>

Ethics

For all their hype and ethical claims, I have sadly found the third sector on many occasions to be deeply unethical in the manner in which staff are treated. This is not always the fault of boards, but the system they find themselves working under and serious lack of resources. Nevertheless the result is the same - the mistreatment of staff in many cases by boards who do not have either the time, resource, experience or sometimes even the motivation to get to know the staff and ensure that they are properly resourced, trained and fairly treated.

Perhaps many small third sector organizations who cannot properly look after their staff due to lack of funding should take the hard decision to either wind up or merge rather than struggle on and risk on-going compromises leading to highly unethical practices.

Many boards – including this one – have no code of conduct for board members, no declaration of interests and no means of disciplining or removing members. Yet they have extensive rules governing their staff's behavior and disciplinary procedures. What does this say about fairness and equality in the third sector?

This organization's practice of maintaining managers – like myself - on part time contracts is in my opinion a classic example of unethical practice.

This board will have to answer as to how they felt their part time manager could accommodate the demands of an organization employing up to 9 staff at one point and latterly with a trading subsidiary to boot. They certainly never imparted this knowledge to me. While they bemoaned the absence of funding that kept me on a part time contract (17.5 hours per week), for most of my time with them they took no action to change the situation and were quite happy to take the benefits of the considerable extra time investment I had to make to manage the organization effectively. (I calculate that I worked an additional 100 days unpaid during my 21 months. For 17 of those 21 months I was paid part time. I was also expected to be available to board members during evenings and weekends).

Competent employers know very well that such jobs as managing staff in a demanding environment can only be properly done on a full time basis and that conscientious managers will end up working many additional hours unpaid to ensure the job is done properly and their credibility is not called into question. In effect the part time manager is manipulated into subsidizing the organization.

To my mind there is a deep disconnect between the good work many third sector organizations set out to do and how they manage themselves internally. This is not true of all in the third sector; some have got it right, but not many in my experience.

I have experienced several diverse third sector organizations in Scotland and Ireland in health, the arts, transport and the environment. This organization is far from unique in grappling with the issues of governance and ethics, but to my mind it should have known better given its experience, its public profile and the claims it makes about its own ethics.

I tell you all this so that you will understand some of the pressures that were at play within this organization and to illustrate how poor governance, poor ethics and limited board capacity can badly damage the growth of an organization with great potential.

As a result of my latest experience I will never again work in the third sector. I have had to accept that the corporate world for all its faults pays more attention to ethics and staff welfare: perhaps because it can afford to. I think this organization's scenario should prompt some searching questions of what the third sector claims to be and what it really is.

I wish you all well. In spite of my traumatic time with this organization I greatly enjoyed working with many of you. I hope we meet again and that your organizations prosper - at no cost to anyone.

Best wishes.

The points made in this letter highlight a number of the limitations of corporate and hierarchical structures of organizational governance. If such structures are to be continued with there will be a requirement for greater transparency and the implementation of improved systems of checks, balances and accountability of board and committee members.

I believe that in the Third Sector there will be an increased demand for greater transparency, more inclusivity and wider representation in management and decision-making. Wise people are creating or restructuring groups and organizations with structures to accomplish these.

The following are ways in which transparency and accountability can be achieved:
    a. Have representatives from all areas involved in decision-making.
    b. Create overlapping circles of information and responsibility.
    c. Have regular consultations with all those involved.
    d. Have managerial discussion and decisions observed by some or all of those involved in the project.

Remember: Seeking opinions from workers and volunteers as well as having an advisory board of skilled and experienced people will widen the available pool of information, experience and expertise.

8

ACQUIRING RESOURCES

It might come as a surprise to find the subject of acquiring resources so far into this book.

I know how important resources are and that the objectives of most projects could not be reached without them. However, the acquisition of resources can feel so essential to groups that they concentrate their efforts on this before being quite clear about what they're attempting to do, how they are going to achieve objectives and how they are going to work, meet, communicate and make decisions together.

My experience is that when the strategies of these are in place the group managing a project is in a better position to ask for support with resources.

> Projects showing clear objectives, workable systems, strong commitment and the evidence of a mutually supportive group culture, stand a better chance of getting the required resources.

Ask for what you need

My great grandmother taught me: 'those who don't ask - don't get!'

And yet, I have met people who believe that because their project is important then whatever is needed will simply turn up. It seems to me to be passive and even somewhat arrogant to assume this and to imagine that little effort needs to be made.

I have heard people described as being good at manifestation. However, I have noticed that those people who seem to have the power of manifestation are very clear about what is needed, have strategies for acquiring it and have the ability to make straightforward requests - often accompanied by some power of persuasion.

> Whatever your project needs, ask for it!

In most situations, there will be at least a 50-50 chance for a positive response. If the answer is yes, be grateful, and if the answer is no, then make sure the door is left open for a change of mind. If the odds seem to be less in your favor then do what you can to improve them. Be enthusiastic about the project. Offer as much detail as is possible about the objectives, how they will be reached and who will be involved.

Exercise your requesting muscles and practice your asking techniques whenever opportunities arise - making sure that those opportunities are convenient to the people you are approaching. People will not usually mind being asked if they see that the project is important and that you are committed to it. Many might feel flattered at being approached. However, do this good-naturedly. Accept refusal with good grace, a smile and acknowledgement of people's time and their willingness to listen to your request. Avoid showing disappointment, disillusionment or resentment at refusals that might make it difficult or even impossible to approach these people again in the future.

> Avoid seeing a refusal as a rejection of the project or of yourself.

Stay positive. Have people around you who will support you in staying positive. Look around for other opportunities.

Being skilled in making requests is usually essential for the success of any voluntary or community project; whether that's in asking for occasional help or for major funding. There ought to be at least one person with this capability in any group.

Fundraising

Raising money for projects can be difficult and may take a lot of time, effort and attention. It's useful to have people in the group who are experienced in creating fundraising events and finding sources of funding.

People with the ability to write successful funding applications are worth their weight in gold.

The following guidelines for filling out a funding application could be useful:

1. Make sure that the project fits the criteria for which the funding is offered.
2. Understand exactly what information the funders require.
3. Know where to place the emphasis in asking for what is needed.
4. Support the application with facts, figures and intended outcomes. These will usually include: the need that will be fulfilled, how and when that will be done, what the outcomes are intended to be, how these will be achieved and how all of this will be measured.
5. Have additional information already formulated in case it is requested.
6. Be certain that your information is correct.
7. Avoid waffling.
8. Write legibly and spell accurately.
9. Keep within the application's guidelines for the number of sheets or the number of words to be used.
10. Check and double-check every detail of the application.
11. Send off the completed application well before the deadline required by the funders. (They may need further information).
12. Have everyone involved hold the vision of the application being successful.
13. Have a letter of acceptance and gratitude already prepared for when the application is approved.

Remember: Have all the data used in all applications readily to hand and keep facts and figures updated.

I have witnessed people attempting to fill in applications without knowing vital facts about their project or where to find this information. Even if one person is responsible for fundraising others ought to be involved and at least know the answers to rudimentary questions and where to find any facts they don't have, such as who were the biggest funders of the project in the previous 3 years and for how much.

Selection processes

I suspect that in coming years it is going to be increasingly difficult to find funding for some community projects, even from traditionally reliable sources. Funding bodies are likely to receive a growing deluge of applications - far greater than the money available. Funders will need to be even more selective than they have been in the past and some of them have already been very selective!

I have witnessed some draconian elimination processes of funding applications. Here is an insight into such selection processes:

Years ago, I attended a workshop on writing successful funding applications that was put on by a major funding agency. I learned that the first part of their selection process was to discard any application that didn't come up to scratch. Poorly written and unclear applications did not make it past this stage. Some applications were not even read beyond the first page. I remember a description of one application that had been dismissed out of hand when three spelling mistakes were discovered in the first few lines. It seemed to have escaped the funder's notice that this application was for capacity building for people in a project run by a group of immigrant women who were most likely poorly educated and whose first language was not English!

It seems probable that, when overwhelmed, even conscientious and compassionate funding bodies may be obliged to find reasons to discard many applications at the first stage. Make certain that yours are not among them! To prevent this, every effort will need to be made to make your application as perfect as possible, to stand out from the rest, to attract the funder's attention and to be irresistible to them.

Differences between the Private and Third Sectors

Private Sector

At the very basic level most business transactions meet the law of supply and demand. In which a demand is identified, or created through marketing, the supply of which is primarily intended to benefit the supplier. In most cases, any real benefit to the consumer is fortuitous, although often of secondary consideration to the supplier. The survival of the business is paramount and will outweigh any other consideration. If a product or service becomes unprofitable, the demand has been inaccurately identified or it becomes obvious that there is a bigger demand for another; then a business will shift its focus to offer goods or services that would bring it higher profitability and lead to its greater sustainability.

The Third Sector

The law of supply and demand in the Voluntary and Community Sector exists, although is sufficiently different to that of the commercial model to require an entirely different approach.

In this sector, initiatives are intended to supply solutions to the demand created by problems and to provide help and support for the identified needs of others. These initiatives are set up for the benefit of those in need. Any type of benefit received by those managing the initiative as a result of their efforts is fortuitous, although secondary to the objectives of the project. While ever the need exists, the organization will endeavor to offer help.

While this may seem to be stating the obvious, the survival instinct is so strong in most of us that this distinction can become blurred. Situations can arise where Third Sector organizations may focus more upon their own sustainability or survival. This often leads to decisions being made for the benefit of the organization rather than the people it was set up to serve. The argument being that if the organization ceases to exist or to continue in its present form then people would not receive the help they need. This kind of shift of focus can be brought about by all kinds of difficulties. However, it most often results from challenges in obtaining resources.

When does the tail wag the dog?

The following story illustrates how quickly this shift in focus can happen:

Julie had been made redundant from her executive post and was discovering that the resulting shock to her self-confidence and self-esteem was blocking her attempts to find another suitable job. While receiving coaching to overcome these blocks and to find a new direction, she realized that she could use this experience to help other people who were in a similar situation.

Julie's research indicated that there was a growing need for some way of supporting some of the skilled and experienced executives and managers who had lost their jobs due to circumstances beyond their control. These circumstances could be financial cuts, changing market forces, the decreased need for their skills or an increased need for skills they didn't currently have. There could be other reasons such as sickness or injury or some change to their personal circumstances.

She began the setting up of a project that would help these people to start over again and support them to overcome their difficulties and find a new and meaningful direction.

Through her own experience it became obvious to Julie that when people were helped to recover from the blow to their self-esteem and from any of their feelings of rejection or betrayal, it would free them to concentrate on finding alternative work with renewed self-confidence. The project was not intended to help people to find jobs, it was to support them to regain their equilibrium and rekindle their previously existing motivation in order for them to turn their lives around.

For some people receiving an income was essential; in which case they would need to look for new paid employment. The people for whom this wasn't the case, such as those with decent redundancy packages or who had been offered early retirement deals, might find new purpose in life by volunteering their extensive experience and valuable skills into the Voluntary and Community sector. In both cases, vital skills and experience would not be lost and people could regain their sense of purpose as they continued to make a useful contribution to society.

The formula first envisaged for the project was one where people would pay for some initial coaching and then would follow a self-coaching program while receiving some occasional experienced supervision and mentoring. They would then offer that same kind of supervision and mentoring based upon their experience of receiving such, to future participants going through the program.

This self-perpetuating, mutually supportive project would require very little outside funding. These days it would probably have been set up as a Social Enterprise, however, as this was in the mid-1990s, that concept did not then exist in the way it does now.

Julie sort help from her friend Dan, a semiretired professional fundraiser, experienced in working with charities. What had been intended to be a self-perpetuating and mutual supporting initiative, was set up instead as a charity with Julie as chairperson/administrator and Dan as secretary/fundraiser. Both of them were to receive some income for their endeavors and, in order to conform with the type of charitable status chosen, the participants of the program would not be obliged to make much, if any, financial contribution towards the help they received because funding would be raised.

After a while it became clear that there was little or no funding for this type of project. The common response to the funding applications being that the intended recipients of the project's support ought to be capable of getting back on their own feet.

This type of response demonstrated a lack of understanding of what happens to people who feel discarded and disempowered within the old paradigm business model. It perpetuated the loss of vital skills and experience and missed the opportunity for turning a problem into a solution.

Dan did discover that there was funding available for supporting long-term unemployed people to find work. The purpose and objectives of the project were changed to meet these funding criteria. Instead of supporting people to once more find roles in business; to start initiatives where they might increase employment opportunities for others, or to offer skills to worthwhile Third Sector groups, the project became devoted to working with long-term unemployed folk, some of whom had a relatively low skill base, or had never had a job and who all lived in a region with few suitable work opportunities.

(I have a huge amount of empathy, concern and compassion for unemployed people who are struggling to find work and who are willing to do whatever is necessary to maintain their financial independence and to provide for their families. I know that in order to fulfill their responsibilities many of these people change their circumstances or set aside their own pride in accepting work that others might consider to be too demeaning, that require too great a shift in attitude or is unacceptable in some way. I believe that these unfortunate people deserve all the support they can get.)

However, the project, as it had been set up, was not designed to provide these people with the type of help they needed. The coaching program had been created for people with quite different experiences around work and sudden unemployment and who required a radically different type of support and motivational coaching. Those involved in delivering the project had no experience of being unemployed for a long time and had no real understanding of the social circumstances of many of the new potential clientele or of the attitudes developed out of those circumstances. Because of this and some other factors, it seemed apparent that the new potential clients were unlikely to receive enough of what they really needed to become permanently employed (assuming that employment existed) and the original clientele, who may have created some solutions to that problem, were forsaken.

As funding was found for several years the project continued for a while during which time some people were helped, I am pleased to say. A good coaching program was delivered on one occasion, although the ongoing mutual support of participants for one another that was first envisioned was not implemented.

The employment situation in the region still has to be adequately addressed.

This story poses a number of questions:
1. In being quick to change the project in order to receive funding, was priority given to the project's survival rather than its stated purpose and objectives?
2. How many creative initiatives never get off the ground or fail to meet their objectives because funders do not see or are not clearly shown the benefits or potential?
3. How many unique projects are modified to fit the criteria of available funding?
4. How many are modified or even hijacked to fit the political needs of the times?
5. How many programs that start out to fulfill some need in others end up being altered to fulfill the needs of the people managing them?
6. In regard to funding, when does the tail end up wagging the dog?

> These may be useful questions for people in community projects to consider. This could be essential if some Social Enterprises become supported financially through investment.

Receiving funding

While there are many difficulties in applying for funding, there can be many pitfalls to receiving it.

The process for getting funding and receiving grants can be a minefield for the unwary. It might be difficult to work out whether or not a project fits the criteria for specific funding. It can sometimes feel almost impossible to comply with restrictions and achieve the required measurement of outcome while delivering a project with good humor and without stress.

> In my experience, some types of funding are not worth the effort.

In some circumstances obtaining funding is a bit like getting a mortgage. The mortgage provider actually owns the property until the mortgage is repaid. A project that is totally dependent upon one or a small number of funders might find most of its decisions being influenced or even dictated by the requirements of those funders.

I have observed situations where groups have been obliged to drastically modify their project, its management and the ways of achieving objectives in order to receive or to maintain funding. Occasionally, this has been to the benefit of all concerned, although, often, it has led to group members feeling impotent, frustrated, disillusioned and dispirited. It might be wise to be aware of what you're giving away in order to receive.

> Some funding opportunities may have strings attached that need to be carefully examined. Very occasionally there might be an agenda behind some offers of funding.

Some of the changes taking place within society, such as increased citizen involvement and empowerment are not to everyone's liking. Wise people holding traditional positions of power, nationally and locally, encourage this involvement. Others do not. Sensible people can see the benefits of projects that are alternative or complimentary to those offered by the establishment. Others might not.

On occasion, an independent project can achieve great success where similar projects within the establishment seem to be less successful. It might be wise for people in such projects to be circumspect about receiving offers of financial support from some sources. There may be need for vigilance when considering funding for projects that some people might consider threaten the status quo.

Here is a cautionary tale:

In Canada in the early 1990s a group of parents who had been homeschooling their children got together to create an independent school for their young teenagers. Some of the parents were teachers and those who were not provided whatever other skills and hands-on work and support that the school needed. They all remortgaged their homes or borrowed money to buy a property in which to house the school.

Together the children and parents ran the school. The children made the decisions about their education with guidance from parents and teachers. Any child could learn whatever subject he or she was keen to learn, regardless of their age, (none of them avoided any of the necessary basic subjects).

If more than six children wanted to study a subject not taught by one of the parents then an appropriate teacher was hired, sometimes for a few hours each week, to cover that subject. For some other subjects the children attended classes in those subjects at local state schools. They paid the fees for those classes.

The children excelled and by the second half of the 1990s several of the pupils under the age of 19 had already attained at least one academic degree.

I discovered the existence of this school when four of the pupils came to a weeklong conference on Ecovillage Development. Because the youngsters didn't have enough money to cover the cost of attending, they offered to pay what they could, camp out, and to engage in work exchange.

The arrangement was that two of them, in rotation, would be in the conference sessions, while, which ever two were not, would help to cook, clean and assist with the administration of the conference by doing such things as the photocopying.

The youngsters attending sessions made notes on their laptops. The results of any activities in which they did not take part were recorded by interviewing those who did. These notes were used in the creation of the Conference Report that was part of their contribution towards the cost of attendance.

These young people seemed to learn more about Ecovillage development than many other attendees of the conference. This information they took home to share with their fellow pupils and no doubt used to good effect in their lives.

These young people were confident, bright, efficient and capable. They were interested in everything. They were good communicators and a joy to be around.

I arranged to visit the school when I was in Canada the following year - I was in for a shock!

I learned that several years previously the Local Authority had informed the school that it was eligible for some financial support to cover the cost of the classes that the youngsters were attending at the local state schools. Over the intervening years this had amounted to a great deal of money. Suddenly, out of the blue, it was revealed that this Authority had discovered an error had been made and that the school was not actually entitled to this financial support.

Any further classes the children attended would once more have to be paid for by them. More seriously, as it was taxpayer's money that had apparently been wrongly allocated, the school was legally obliged to repay every cent. In spite of great efforts in challenging this decision, it was upheld and a deadline imposed.

There was no way that the fundraising options available could raise the amount to be repaid in time. All the parents involved were already stretched to their financial limit, which made further borrowing impossible. With so much stacked against them, including potential litigation, the decision was made by parents and pupils to sell the school property to cover the cost of the required repayment.

After much soul-searching, it was agreed that without the building and because of the levels of stress being experienced by those involved, including the youngsters, it was not possible to continue. The school was closed down.

> From this I have learned there may be occasions when it's wise to look a gift horse in the mouth!

Borrowing

Projects that will generate funds through their activities may be able to borrow money needed for startup or development.

Although traditional banks are usually reluctant to lend to those organizations that are attempting to deal with escalating social issues, there are some banks that are opening up loan finance to give these organizations the tools with which to help themselves.

One such bank in the UK is Charity Bank, the social savings bank that has supported such organizations across the UK since 2002. It invests all of its money in charities and other organizations whose mission is to improve the community or the environment. Details of all investments are published and depositors are not only kept informed, they are encouraged to actively engage with the recipients of Charity Bank loans.

Another UK bank that makes loans available to some charities and local projects is the Co-operative Bank, which is customer-centric and member-led. The Co-operative Bank's Ethical Policy, which has existed since 1992, ensures that it will always stand up for the issues that customers feel passionate about. Customers have a say in what is done with their money and on the issues that matter to them, such as human rights, animal welfare, fair trade and care for the environment. The customer/members also share in profits the bank makes. There are similar banks in other countries.

More people are beginning to realize that there is an alternative to depositing their savings in the main High Street commercial banks, where they will have no idea what use their money is put to. More of us are moving our money to where we believe it could do some good, such as the banks already mentioned. This does not only apply to banks. Some of those wanting to have their money used for the benefit of local people are placing their funds in local Credit Unions. An increasing number of people are investing their money in such regulated institutions as Savings and Loan Organizations and Industrial and Provident Societies.

Community financing

In the community in which I lived in Scotland, working with the support and guidance of the Financial Services Authority, we created Ekopia - our Community Resource Exchange. Formed as an Industrial and Provident Society and Social Enterprise this has provided the mechanism for local investment opportunities.

Through Ekopia, finance has been raised for the construction of a Wind Park, the Community cooperative buyout of the local shop and its development into the Phoenix Community Stores, 2 cafes and a bakery. There have been other loans for many more community projects, large and small, including the independent Steiner School. Through having this mechanism in place, and with Ekopia as a founding member of Development Trusts, grants have been made available to the Community for such things as affordable housing.

It has been a joy to see how this local financial initiative has improved economic sustainability and helped the Community to flourish. For information on the varied work and achievements of Ekopia visit: www.ekopia-findhorn.org

There are a variety of examples of similar local and national financial organizations around the world. In New Zealand for example there is Prometheus Finance, a Qualifying Financial Entity (QFE) that was established in 1983 as a Charitable Trust following the example set by a number of social-finance organizations in Europe. Prometheus lends to a range of sectors and activities throughout New Zealand ranging from renewable energy, through sustainable agriculture and energy-efficient housing, to resource recovery and habitat protection.

These and many other types of institutions may be willing to loan to Charities, Associations and projects that can clearly show that they can fulfill the conditions of the loan.

Complementary currencies

There is now a growing movement in many countries towards the creation of local community currencies. These, in complementing national currencies and other forms of barter and exchange, are supporting individuals and communities to become more self-sustaining.

In complementary currency schemes, money is exchanged for notes, vouchers, tokens or whatever you prefer to call them, usually of equal value, which can be spent with any participating individual or business member in the scheme. Usually, each issue has a limited lifetime and the end date is printed on each one. At that time they can be redeemed for money to the same value or exchanging for notes in the next issue.

In 2003, through Ekopia, and with further assistance from the FSA, our community created a local complementary currency - The Eko. The community has now enjoyed the benefits of four issues. This has encouraged trading within the Community and with the other individuals and businesses in the local area that wished to participate. These include pubs, cafes, B&Bs, taxi services, trades and professional people. This means that money exchanged for Ekos, that can only be spent locally, remains in the area for the benefit of local people.

> If there is no such system within your local community perhaps you and others could start one.

Being creative

The fall-out from the banking crisis in 2008 has gravely affected international, national, regional and local governments. Many of them have needed to reduce their budgets for public health care, education and the variety of forms of social care in which they are engaged. These have been undergoing radical changes. This has seriously impacted the Voluntary and Community sector and is likely to do so for some time to come.

In recent times, sensible, proactive and caring people have often stepped into the breach to fulfill some need that is being ignored or inadequately covered by the state. It is apparent that much more of this is going to be required in the foreseeable future.

> It seems clear that a decreasing amount of funding is going to be chased by an increasing number of Voluntary and Community Groups. This is obviously not sustainable. It is clearly time to think outside the box.

So many people have become fixated on money as being the most important commodity on the planet, and believe that it is what is required to make anything happen. It ain't necessarily so!

> Surely, money is a means to an end and that end might be achieved by all manner of means!

Asking is one way. Sometimes there is no need to raise the money to buy what is needed. People providing the commodities or services may be willing to donate some of whatever is needed to a project, if asked directly.

Another way is through exchange.

Exchange

In many community projects great efforts are made to raise the money to pay for goods and services needed to reach the project's objectives. Do all of those goods and services actually need to be exchanged for money? Some do of course, and yet, perhaps not as many as we might think. Within a group or project there may be many things that could be exchanged for other things.

All over the world an enormous amount of local trading is now being carried out through some kind of exchange or barter. In this way people who are without much money are able to improve some quality of their lives. To support this there are a variety of exchange mechanisms in operation around the planet. These systems allow people to exchange the skills and commodities that they have for the skills and commodities that they need:

  a. LETS (Local Exchange Trading Systems): www.gmlets.u-net.com and www.letslinkuk.net.
  b. Time Banking: http://www.timebanking.org
  c. Green Dollars.
  d. Green Pounds.

Regardless of what these systems are called, most operate in a similar a fashion. Time, skills, services and commodities of every description are exchanged for something other than money.

> If any of these systems are available in your area, join them. If none exist, then perhaps you or others could start one.

Even without an organized local system, some Voluntary and Community Groups could perhaps operate a form of regular or irregular exchange amongst themselves. There may be skills within one group that could be exchanged for something that another group has in surplus. Some groups have easy access to some things that others don't. How can these be exchanged? What skills and time; the hire of rooms, equipment and vehicles could be offered up for exchange?

The number of potentially exchangeable items might only be limited by the imagination. Within any group of people there are likely to be a multiplicity of skills and commodities that could be used for exchange. It might be interesting to conduct an exercise within your group to discover what is available. One group of people with whom I conducted this experiment filled four sheets of Flipchart paper (in small writing) with their ideas.

Make a note

Make a note of the skills and experience and the surplus item that your project could offer in exchange for things you need.

What about pooling resources? Does every group have to own all of its equipment? How about a number of groups getting together to purchase photocopying machines, minivans and the like? Some communities have created projects to make equipment available to community groups. Some of these are publicly funded and some are not.

Of course, such pooling and sharing requires that people communicate clearly with one another; make and keep agreements; take responsibility for caring for equipment and be understanding and supportive towards one another.

Hurray! This also provides opportunities to meet other wonderful people, to discover what good things others are doing and how they are also endeavoring to make a difference.

9

PROJECT MEASUREMENT, EVALUATION, REFLECTION, REVIEW AND FEEDBCK

These are essential to ensure that any project is achieving its desired objectives; that the systems, procedures and processes are being appropriately effective and that people in receipt of the project's work are benefiting from it and are happy with what they are receiving.

Things do go wrong from time to time. The trick is to notice when this is happening, investigate what is going wrong and to immediately take action to put things right.

Often the cause for things to stop functionally in the way envisioned is lack of funding, although by no means always. Beware of throwing more money at a problem that could better be solved by some careful consideration.

Measurement and Evaluation

If your project were intended to bring about a change, to make a difference to people or to a situation, it would be wise to consider the following questions:

Q

1. How will you know how effective you are being?
2. How will you establish what effect your project is having on raising awareness or if thoughts and opinions have been changed by your efforts?
3. How will you measure progress and success?

Measuring progress isn't always a high priority at the start of a project. However, creating simple and straightforward ways of gathering data will not only help with monitoring and measuring progress, it can be included in funding applications used to encourage support.

> It would be wise to keep a record of all the project's activities and events.

Options:
a. You could record the number of people who were involved in projects and what the outcomes are.
b. Project working groups could be asked to record information that emerges from their work.
c. It could also be interesting and useful to make a photographic record of your progress.
d. To avoid wasting time and resources it would sensible to have ways for monitoring results of trainings and on the introduction of new systems or processes to check for their effectiveness. This could be achieved through surveys and by requesting and recording feedback from those involved.

Reflection and Review

In all the activities involved in keeping a project moving forward and doing interesting and exciting things, it is easy to forget to ask if the project is moving in the right direction and in a supportive and functional way.

> Having regular times to reflect and to ask 'How are we doing?' is an essential safety check.

Opportunities for reflection and reviews can be held regularly for the group to monitor the progress of the project as well as for individuals to review their personal work, achievements and satisfaction.

Reflection and review upon progress

Regular opportunities for reflection and review on progress, of working practices, systems and procedures will help the group to remain effective and relevant. These are useful when those in the project need to make an assessment of their achievements and progress.

Q Questions could be asked such as:
a. How on track are we with our objectives?
b. Name some of the achievements that have furthered the aims of the group/projects purpose.
c. How effective is the process on…?
d. What is the most important achievement since the last review/meeting?
e. What has worked well?
f. What has not worked so well?
g. What could be done differently in the future and what new or different steps could be taken?

Individuals can reflect upon and review their personal work and contribution to the project through these and similar questions. Reviews provide opportunities for people to acknowledge one another for work well done and for efforts made.

The number of questions in a review will depend upon the circumstances and the number of people present. In a small meeting each person present can answer these questions in one Go-Round. In larger events, these could be considered in small groups.

> As well as a way of evaluating work, progress and interactions, a few minutes could be provided at the end of meetings, activities, discussions and decisions to discuss how effective were the processes for these or how they could be improved upon.

Reflection and review on objective, values and ethics

A reflection and review would be useful for assessing in what ways the objectives are being met and how the agreed Values and Ethics are influencing the behavior and working practices of individuals and of the outcomes of activities.

When things go wrong in projects it may be because some people have got their wires crossed about the objectives of that project. The values and ethics of some of the staff and volunteers might be at odds with those stated for the project.

Consider some of the following questions:

Q
1. Are the aims and objective that people have 'signed up to' being pursued?
2. Does it seem that the project is veering away from what people believe to be the objectives and towards something that they are not committed to?
3. Are the values and ethics of the project being implemented?
4. Are these still compatible with those of the individuals involved?
5. Has something in the project changed since these people felt inspired to become part of it?
6. Has something in them changed since they joined the project?

Working together to identify the answers and deal with the responses to these questions could alleviate the current problems and save time and effort later down the track.

Reflection and review on interactions and working relationships

In my experience, dissatisfaction with the work, uncomfortable working relationships, dysfunctional systems, lack of comprehension of how staff and volunteers need to be supported and managed, and little understanding of the development of groups and their culture are the reasons why many projects fail, why volunteers leave a project or stop volunteering altogether.

One of the challenges of working in projects is that they tend to be full of other people!

The staff and volunteers in projects are often made up of people from very different backgrounds and who have different approaches to life and ways of working from one another. Whatever activity people engage in they bring their whole selves to it. They bring their personality, their characteristics, their patterns of behavior, the pain of their past and the hopes for their future. This hope for the future may be the very reason some people volunteer in a particular project.

A wage packet or the prospect of promotion might compensate for difficulties with colleagues or managers that can arise in paid employment in projects. What compensation is there for volunteers within projects for putting up with difficulties with colleagues?

Often the common ground shared by all, the concern, the cause, the reason for people to choose to work in or to volunteer their time to a project, is enough to hold them together and to work out differences or difficulties. Sometimes, it is not.

If there are relationship problems between volunteering colleagues, or/and employed staff of a project it could be worthwhile dealing with those problems rather than risk the loss of valuable people. This will provide people with opportunities for personal development. Difficulties between people are rarely all one sided, although they may seem that way from each person's perspective! Using conflict or disharmony as an opportunity for self-exploration can be very rewarding.

Sometimes the people with whom we have the most difficulty turn out to offer our biggest opportunity for self-awareness and self-improvement.

Choosing not to examine the part we might each play in an uncomfortable relationship could be a lost opportunity to know ourselves better. Believing that everybody else is at fault is likely to be an illusion. Any unresolved situation in a project you choose to leave might very well reappear in any future project you choose to join.

A reflection and review would be useful for assessing the quality of interactions between people and in what ways these are affecting the activities and outcomes of the project.

Q

This review would enquire into:
a. What has been the most enjoyable aspect of our working together?
b. What has been difficult?
c. How constructive are communications between us?
d. What is one thing that needs more attention paying to it while working together?

To create items for discussion a single word could be asked that would describe areas for review. These could be such things as: communication, co-operation, resources, or timing. Review any relevant items under each heading.

Reflection and review on volunteering

Having capable and willing volunteers is obviously essential to all Voluntary Projects. It is also vital to the survival of so many Community projects.

If people feel unfulfilled, dissatisfied or irritated with their volunteer work then perhaps they haven't found the right fit. They might be a square peg in a round hole or their expectations, theirs or other peoples, may have been too high. It may be because they feel underused and undervalued.

Volunteering ought to be fulfilling. Even though some of the work may be tedious, tiring, challenging, occasionally uncomfortable and sometimes downright dirty, there needs to be some sense of achievement at the end of it.

On the occasions when volunteering does not seem to be working well within a project for some of the following reasons:
- Some of the volunteer's hearts may no longer be in the project.
- Some of the volunteers might not be adequately trained or managed.
- Some of the volunteers could be square pegs in round holes.
- Some of the volunteers may have unrealistically high expectations of themselves, of others or of the role they are playing.
- Other people may have unrealistic expectations of some of the volunteers.
- Some of the volunteer's skills might be underused or undervalued.

It would be beneficial to spend some time reflecting upon and reviewing the current volunteering situation through the perspective of each of these points. Helping volunteers in checking their current experience against what they set out to achieve with their volunteering and what they hoped to receive from it would be a beneficial thing to do.

Q

This review could consider questions such as:
a. How well are volunteers fitted to their roles or tasks?
b. Is their training adequate?
c. Are their skills being appreciated and appropriately used?
d. How well are volunteers being supported to do their work?
e. What do they need to become even more effective?
f. Are people feeling fulfilled through volunteering in this project?
g. What do they require or need to happen for them to feel so?

Reflection and review on next steps

Having reflected and reviewed all these aspects of the project, it would be wise to identify the next steps to be taken to deal with or improve these situations and to move the project forward in the most appropriate ways.

Q **Questions:**
1. What steps could be taken to move forward with what has been identified?
2. What will you/we do differently from now on?
3. What changes will you/we now make as a result of what we have learned?
4. What contribution will you/we now make towards fulfilling the agreements that have come out of this review?
5. How will we recognize when those changes have been made?

These sorts of questions can bring further clarity and may provide an obvious forward direction. They can assist in reinforcing key elements of a reviewed issue and can encourage commitment to action.

Review processes and many more useful questions for a variety of situations are among the processes described in the books ENJOYABLE AND EFFECTIVE MEETINGS and EFFORTLESS FACILITATION in the YOU MAKE THE DIFFERENCE series available from Amazon and accessible through our website: www.youmakethedifference.net/books

On Track Review

Projects can lose momentum and become ineffective when the people managing them do not pay enough attention to keeping aligned with the purpose and objectives. When those involved do not recognize or admit to one another that they are off course for achieving the goals and objectives of the project, this might result in loss of support from elsewhere. The On Track Review is useful for checking these out.

After the current reality has been honestly recognized then work can be done on identifying what the ideal situation might be and how to get from what currently exists to that on track ideal in the most effective and mutually supportive manner.

Applications
This process is useful in a number of situations:
1. If the project seems to be off track.
2. To review progress at the end of the year or some other significant period.
3. In preparation for the Annual General meeting.
4. When a project seems to be losing effectiveness.
5. When a project is in some kind of difficulty.
6. As a preparation for an application for major funding.

7. When an organization is making a significant change such as applying for charitable status.

If a large number of people participate, this process can be conducted in common interest groups such as departments within an organization or the stakeholder groups who would be affected by the outcome.

Outside Facilitation
This could be an event that would benefit from outside facilitation. If that is not possible then several group members working together could facilitate it.

On-track Review process

Step 1. Stating the purpose
The purpose and aims of the organization, group or project as currently stated are written up on a board or flip chart that is visible to everyone. This might reveal that some people involved have not been completely clear about the purpose of the project or the aims of the group. In rare cases this could show that the purpose and aims have never been clearly defined, in which case some work will obviously need to be done on that before moving to step 2.

Step 2. Visualization
Working alone, each participant visualizes the best setup they can imagine to fulfill the project's purpose as stated. Visualizing the Ideal Day within the organization or project is an effective process to use for this.

Ideal Day Process
The participants write down everything they would want to happen during an ideal day in the organization, group or project in order to be on track to achieve its stated objectives. They are to put in every exquisite detail they can think of in the areas posed by the following questions:

Q

a. What activities would be engaged in?
b. Who would be engaged in them?
c. Where would these activities take place?
d. What facilities, equipment, resources and support would ideally be available for these activities?
e. How would it feel to work in these circumstances?
f. What would be the ideal outcome of these activities?

g. Anything else?

These questions are each addressed as the Ideal Day is described as though it is a diary of the events throughout one day. Starting with the moment of approach the building or first task of the day and ending when there is nothing else to be done on that day.

This process can help to widen thinking. For this reason, I would recommend that in their imaginations, people would consider there to be no restrictions of time or money in the creation of their Ideal Day.

If it can be imagined, it can happen in this Ideal Day.

Does someone want to take a planeload of food to Africa? No problem, they can do that and be back in time for lunch. Do they want to have a famous film star launch a project? Easy, they just imagine that person doing so. People can allow their imaginations to go as wild as possible.

> This is not the time for limited thinking or self-censorship. Some of the more outlandish ideas can be used as metaphors later in the process. If people tell themselves something is silly or not possible, they ought to write it down anyway.

Everything is written about in glowing, positive terms: the sights, sounds and smells, the colors, the atmosphere and the attitudes of the people.

AVK

There are reasons for being aware of the sights, sounds, smells and colors when visualizing an Ideal Day. As was covered earlier we are each usually predominately Auditory, Visual or Kinesthetic in our mode of learning and experiencing. The use of each of the senses while creating the Ideal Day will help to make the visualized activities stronger and more memorable, regardless through which of those modes each person best receives information. It is especially important to remember this when taking groups of people through this exercise because they are likely to have their imaginations triggered differently from one another.

Remembering that the aim is to identify the ideal circumstances through which the project could achieve its goals, each imaginary Ideal Day is to be full, rich, interesting, exciting and joy filled. If it is not like that, it needs to be re-thought.

From experience, I recommend that participants are encouraged to keep writing from the start, regardless of what comes into their minds, rather than spending time pondering or getting their thoughts in some order. A useful trick is to keep the pen point on the paper. This seems to help to keep thoughts flowing.

Step 3. Sharing the day
The group or groups now reform for everyone to take a turn in reading out their Ideal Day to everyone else in their group. Each Ideal Day description is to be listened to with respect and encouragement. It is important that no derisory remarks or negative comments are made by any of the listeners. The contents of each person's Ideal Day are indications of the dreams that this person has for the potential of the organization, group or project. Not only that, many of these descriptions will be used as metaphors and symbols for what could be made possible.

> At the end of each person's story their contribution is to be applauded by everyone in the group with delighted enthusiasm and appreciation.

A synopsis of what is said is written up on a board, although no names of who said them are indicated.

Step 4. Finding the common ground
Through a process to identify common ideals through linking similar ideas and grouping related ideals together, a picture will emerge of the ideal circumstances for continuing to carry out the objectives of the organization, group or project.

This is also the time to consider the metaphors and symbols represented by some of the ideals. Most of the seemingly unrealistic ideas can be seen as metaphors or symbols for changes that could be realized. For example, a lavish party at the end of the day could represent a need for more celebrations, social interaction or perhaps to feel more valued and appreciated. The dream of going to Paris for lunch might indicate a desire for some mutual leisure engagements or perhaps more adventurous food in the cafeteria. The more outlandish ideals like food planes to Africa and stars to open projects might indicate a need for more direct action or ambitious thinking.

Step 5. What already exists?

Now that people have identified their ideals for achieving the organization, group or project's purpose it is the time to look at what currently exists.

Working alone once more each person recalls an actual day in the life of the group, project etc. that they experienced some time in the recent past. It is useful if the day chosen has some aspects to it that were of concern or that did not turn out so well. To obtain the widest possible snapshot of the life of the group etc., it is important for each person to choose their own specific day, not one dictated by the facilitator.

Everyone writes down all the details of the happenings of their chosen day exactly in the way they experienced it. As with the Ideal Day, this is written down in diary form and every detail is recorded, including the outcomes of any decisions and actions and the feelings that the person experienced. This part of the process is about being realistic, not creative. It is to bring out into the open what already works and what doesn't work so well in fulfilling the organization, group or project's purpose.

> It is imperative that all information is included. That opinions and thoughts about what works and what does not work well are based upon people's experience.

This is a good way to remember the things that work well in the organization, the things to be proud of. This is an opportunity to be realistic about what doesn't work so well in the project, things to be less proud of.

Although it is vital for people to be honest, it is not about blaming the system or shaming any individuals. It is not about bemoaning the lack of funding or railing against an unjust world. It is about identifying and recording the details of what actually happens day to day.

To prevent it from becoming a depressing or chastening exercise, the facilitator manages this in a light manner. Perhaps lightening the mood by bringing gentle humor in where appropriate.

Step 6. Sharing the reality

As before, everyone then shares with one another what she or he has written down. This is a vital part of the process that allows everyone to hear and acknowledge what really goes on from personal experience rather than from the perspective of gossip, or rumor.

It might be uncomfortable for some people to speak about or to hear things that might be considered negative. Even so, it is vital to do so. If the pitfalls in previous thinking, current initiatives or ideas for potential projects are not identified, then whatever problems or dysfunctional systems or behavior that already exist in the organization, group or project, are likely to be perpetuated. This is the ideal time and process for the recognition of those potential pitfalls to come to light.

As before, a synopsis is written on a board. Common themes will probably appear as the areas of related experiences are linked. Others can now be explored.

Step 7. Getting from here to there

By now, how close to or how far from being on track for the project achieving the highest ideal objectives will have become clear. Perhaps the gap is encouragingly small. Maybe it is alarmingly very wide. The areas that require work will have become apparent.

It is time to consider how to get from where the organization, group or project currently is, to where it now clearly and ideally would wish to be. The questions to ask are:

Q

1. How on track are we?
2. Which parts of the shared ideal are already in place?
3. What parts of the current reality need to be improved?
4. Ought any of these to be discarded altogether?
5. How to fill in the remaining gaps?
6. What new and revolutionary ideas identified in the ideals can be initiated to move us forward to a new and more ideal way of being on track?
7. How can we do that simply and mutually supportively?

This is the time for participants to inspire and empower each other.

Step 8. Working Groups

After identifying these ideas, working groups can now be set up to pursue them. If this is a full day event then this work, or at least some of it, can be carried out immediately; otherwise future meetings will need to be set up. A careful record ought to be kept of who will do what and by when and how these will be reported back to all those who have participated in this event.

> Note: It is important that everyone involved in the process so far is included or suitably represented in these ongoing discussions and decisions to prevent feelings of exclusion and any potential for undermining or sabotaging the outcomes.

Ending process
A suitable ending process such as a Go-Round will allow participants to share their thoughts and feelings about the event with everyone in the group or in their new working group. If time is short then a Paired Sharing will give them the opportunity to share with at least one other person.

Closure
The facilitator sums up the process, reiterates the decisions taken, clarifies the work to be done in the working groups and announces the date of the next follow-on meeting at which the working groups will report progress.

Appreciations all round. Close.

Feedback

Feedback is an important source of information. It enables people in a project to learn firsthand about its effectiveness or otherwise and to discover what is working well and what is not.

Receiving feedback
There are two ways of receiving feedback - directly and indirectly.

Indirect feedback
This is delivered gradually over time as people don't carry out their roles effectively, there is discontent and disharmony within the group, people leave and projects fail.

> This kind of feedback is inevitable if issues are ignored in the vain hope of avoiding criticism and conflict or facing problems that might be difficult to deal with.

By putting off or avoiding dealing with difficulties; in not setting up simple means for those involved to give direct and regular feedback to management or to one another, people in projects can create the very situations that are trying to be avoided.

The antidote to this is to have regular opportunities for direct feedback built into the culture of the group and project.

Feedback Questionnaires
A common practice is for the use of questionnaires for review and evaluation and especially as methods for receiving feedback. This written

form may be a requirement by those to whom the group is accountable or to be used as a way to follow-up on decisions and actions.

Some thoughts on preparing questionnaires have been covered in an earlier section. It can be useful to have a practice run to trial questionnaires to ensure that they make sense and really will provide the key information required.

Sometimes questionnaires require no signature and so some people might use this anonymity for making criticism or expressing opinions that they do not have to stand behind or explain to anyone. While this is a way to receive information that might not otherwise be forthcoming this seems to be less than desirable in community projects and mutually supportive groups. I think this creates a lost opportunity for people to take responsibility for what they say and for all those involved to hear perspectives that may be similar to or quite different from their own.

Because questionnaires need to be written, reproduced, handed out, collected in, read, recorded and probably filed away, in some circumstances, such as having small numbers of personnel available, they might be more trouble than they are worth.

Complaints

> Many people fear complaints because they think they are indications of failure. And yet, in most cases, complaints are valuable feedback.

People who complain are offering very clear feedback about something they are unhappy with. Complaints are opportunities rather than problems, unless they are unheard, ignored or not remedied.

Obviously, it would be better if there is no cause for complaint in the first place and of course there are people for whom complaining is a way of life. In these cases complaints may emerge as grumble or gossip. Even so, there is maturity and wisdom in seeing complaints as opportunities to improve working practices and offer better service.

> You could make the difference by helping project members to turn any of their complaints into direct feedback that can be clearly received and appropriately acted upon.

Direct feedback

Direct feedback is when the people involved in a project are able to express concerns, talk about progress of how things are working or not, and what they are thinking and feeling about things directly with one another and the people who can do something about the relevant situations.

10

IT IS OVER WHEN IT IS OVER

The topics covered in this book will go a very long way towards creating and maintaining successful groups and projects. Even so, the saying: "all good things come to an end", is sometimes the case in even the most worthwhile and successful projects.

I believe there is a myth regarding sustainability. For some people, sustainability has come to mean ensuring the continued existence of something at all costs, regardless of the quality of that existence or of its remaining relevance. There are some occasions when the time, effort and resources required to sustain a project far outweigh the benefits that a project can continue to offer. Occasionally, situations will occur, sometimes quite unexpectedly, which make it impossible or perhaps unnecessary for a project to continue.

Projects come to an end for all sorts of reasons:
a. The reasons for the project coming into being may no longer exist.
b. There might be a lack of resources. Projects that depend upon funding may be able to continue for quite a while, and yet there may come a time when a project ceases to attract the funding that it needs to continue effectively.
c. The people involved in a project might move away, experience a change of circumstances or even a change of mind.
d. People can lose energy or interest in any project, especially one that

seems to be a continuous uphill struggle. Even the most dedicated people can grow weary.
e. A project or a group that no longer has relevance, especially to the majority of its members, is likely to become increasingly difficult and frustrating to work in.
f. Projects can lose momentum, may become ineffective or lose support because the people in them have not recognized or admitted to themselves that they have already achieved their purpose or that circumstances have changed or they are no longer necessary or relevant in their current form.

Through participating in a relevance evaluation process people in a group, project or organization can evaluate the current and future relevance. Through this it might become recognized that the project has completed its purpose, aims and objectives.

Relevance Review

After stating the purpose and aims of the project, the incisive question to ask could be:

Q

'If this organization/group/project did not exist, would we want or need to invent it, if so, for what exact purpose and why?'

This is a time for courage and honesty. It might not be easy for those involved to recognize that their group, project or organization may no longer have real relevance as it currently exists or that it may need to be rethought or restructured to have continued relevance.

> The most valuable people in the group could be the ones willing to speak the uncomfortable truths.

Responding to 'Yes'

If the majority of people involved feel that the answer to the above question of relevance is 'yes', then the group may choose to go through the steps of visualizing the ideal set up, identifying the current reality and working out how to bridge the gap between the two in order to become even more effective, productive and relevant in the future. The Ideal Day process described earlier could be useful for this.

Responding to 'No'

If the answer is 'no' then the group could spend the rest of the event considering how best to proceed.

Some suggested options:
a. The group considers a new project to which they and their resources could be dedicated.
b. The group makes plans to initiate an Action Search process to identify one or more projects in which to become involved. (This process is one of the readymade meeting designs described in EFFORTLESS FACILITATION in this series.)
c. The group initiates the winding up of the group or the project.

This relevance process may not be easy to conduct if disharmony in the group is common or if the leader or other people engaged in the project want to retain control. If people are desperate to hang on to their roles or to the very existence of the project, regardless of its ineffectiveness or irrelevance or even having successfully completed its purpose, then this process may be impossible to initiate. This could be unfortunate because these are the very situations where this process is most needed.

An inspiring outcome from a Relevance Review:

A group had for some time been doing excellent pioneering work on recycling in their local area. As their work proved to be successful and public opinion towards recycling improved, the Local Authority created a comprehensive recycling collection system, which effectively made much of the group's work redundant.

Instead of rejoicing in their victory of achieving widespread recycling in their area, the group hung on to their need for existence. In their reluctance to admit to their current situation and apparent irrelevance the group spent its time criticizing the way the local authority was managing the recycling.

A Relevance Review helped them to see that their original purpose had been successfully completed. This then left them free to make new choices.

They decided to reorganize the group to become more specialized. Some of the group chose to research the recycling of difficult items such as batteries and used engine oil. Some looked for ways to encourage people to purchase items that had been repaired or recycled and other members were interested in promoting approaches to saving energy and resources. These were ideal projects for a volunteer group to engage in, especially in times of financial constraints when there is little money available to pay people to do this kind of work. The group discovered that in its new way of working it had become more relevant than ever.

Leadership: Stepping up or stepping down

At this stage in a projects life, it might be the time for the leader to step up to their responsibility of holding the group together as it shakes itself into the best new format; with the most suitable systems and methods for achieving its purpose. It may take strength and courage to stay in the role at this time.

On the other hand, this might be the time for a leader to step down. Perhaps the person currently leading the group or who has led the group from the beginning might no longer be the most appropriate leader. Maybe the group now needs a leader with different skills and abilities. The qualities of leadership that it takes to launch an initiative or to start a group, may not be the ones needed to sustain it or change it or to maintain group harmony and cohesiveness through those changes.

It could be that the leader has been inspiring the group and holding it together until the next appropriate leader could emerge.

> The wise leader knows when it is time for someone else to take on the leadership role. In this case it may take strength and courage to step down.

Winding up

If, for whatever reason, the decision is taken to wind up the project, it is important that this is done with care and awareness. There are some practical things that need to be addressed regarding assets and commitments when a project is coming to an end.

If the current project group feels unable to continue, and there is still a need for the service it has been providing, perhaps there is another group that could take over some of that work? Would that be the appropriate group to make best use of any remaining assets? Might those in the group who would like to continue to be supportive to this cause find a place in this group to which they could offer their experience?

Remaining assets will need to be appropriately distributed or disposed of. Any that have been acquired through public funding or other forms of fundraising will need to be offered to other appropriate community projects. All this must be fully documented.

Dealing with the feelings

> During the final stages it is important that all those involved in the project continue to be supportive to one another.

It is likely that some people may feel disappointed in the decision to close down. Their feelings will need to be acknowledged. It can be difficult and even painful to wind up a project, especially if it is dear to people's hearts and there is some continuing belief in a need for such work.

Closing down a project might bring with it a sense of failure or embarrassment, particularly if it has had a high profile. There may be feelings of resentment towards those people, inside or outside of the group, whose actions are perceived to have been the cause of the closure. Even those people who believe, as I do, that there is no such thing as failure – only opportunities through which to learn – may find it will require a great deal of strength to keep an open heart towards some people in these circumstances.

It is important to have a review process through which to reflect upon achievements and to recognize successes.

> It could be enormously beneficial to have a completion process to provide those involved with an opportunity to acknowledge one another's effort and commitment and to offer appreciation for work well done and especially for attitudes of care and support.

Details for managing Completion Processes are described in our book EMPOWERING VOLUNTEER MANAGEMENT in this series that is available on Amazon and accessible through:
www.youmakethedifference.net/books

Celebrate

> At the end of any project it is important for there to be an attitude of celebration of successes achieved and appreciation of all who have been involved.

The more successful a project has been the more cause there would seem for celebration. However, even when a project has been less effective than intended or has been closed prematurely, for whatever reason, there are still things that can be celebrated:
- The work that has been effective.
- Those occasions when everything ran smoothly.
- The coming together of the people in the group.
- All the things that have been learned.
- The opportunities for fun, inspiration and the personal development of those involved.

Mark the end of your project with whatever type of celebration feels appropriate.

Options:
a. A goodbye party.
b. A potluck supper.
c. Have everyone in the group go out for lunch.
d. At the very least, arrange for a special cake.
e. Cards and small gifts might be exchanged among the group too.

Engaging in a comprehensive completion and celebration can help keep the door open to opportunities for people involved in this project to engage with one another in future projects.

Remember, out of this ending, there may come new beginnings. There is plenty of work that needs to be done out there!

People Power

It's clear that decisions made by a relatively few powerful or influential people - altruistic or self-interested – often still do not properly address the needs and concerns of the majority of people struggling to make their lives work in the face of social, environmental and economic dysfunction.

> It makes far more sense for the people who are most effected to have a say in what is needed, to have a voice in the decision-making and a hand in the required actions.

Many people are no longer prepared to put up with social situations that do not serve them well. They are increasingly dissatisfied with the decisions that affect their lives that are made by others who have not taken their concerns, needs and views into consideration.

The cultural and social changes being experienced in many places around the world have created the necessity for increased community engagement. This has provided opportunities for people to recreate their communities in the way of their own choosing.

> Many community groups and projects are now contributing to one of the most significant social changes to take place in recent times. This is the ever-increasing numbers of citizens becoming proactively involved in projects to improve their local communities in villages, towns and city districts.

People are no longer feeling powerless to influence the future of the areas in which they live. They are getting together, in groups large or small, to bring about the changes they desire to see in their societies. More and more people are willing to become involved in community projects and are stepping up to take some responsibility for making beneficial things happen.

This is rarely done in isolation. Just at the time when it is important for people to become engaged in creating the future they wish to see, there are systems available which can help:

a. Ready-made mechanisms for sharing information and offering mutual support.
b. There are many individuals, groups and organizations with expertise and experience in community processes that can assist.
c. There are networks, local national and global, through which useful information can be shared.
d. There are movements such as Transition Towns, who offer information and tried and trusted formulas and models for community regeneration and particularly for increased local environmental sustainability: http://www.transitionnetwork.org.

The regeneration of a community requires involvement, input, discussion and decision-making by as wide a range of the community's citizens as possible. Community groups and organizations that have been formed for specific purposes can carry out many, and in some cases, most of the necessary activities, services and projects within a community.

Sensible community groups will have an awareness of what other community groups are doing and will have the intention of being mutually supportive to one another.

Revolution or Evolution

There are now a great many examples of fledgling or successful community led regeneration in all parts of the world. This grassroots movement is expanding exponentially. I heard this recently described as potentially the greatest social revolution that humanity has seen.

> I do not see it as a revolution; I believe it is an inevitable step in human evolution!

It seems to me that increased community engagement and more management of society at the local level is the next obvious evolutionary step in humanity's ways of coexistence. As with all forms of evolution this starts with tiny changes that are improvements on what was there before, have been passed on and become integrated. The difference between this human evolutionary step and all previous ones is that this one is being made very consciously.

As with all evolutionary steps, the timing of this one is perfect. Just as we human beings are waking up to our potential for creating a future together at a local and community level, we have all the information, technology and support that we need to do so. There is a wealth of ideas and experiences available on what could be done to create vibrant, sustainable and enjoyable communities and on how that might be achieved.

A lot of information, methods, processes and tools for this are in the book INSPIRING COMMUNITY SUSTAINABILITY in the YOU MAKE THE DIFFERENCE series, which is available from Amazon and accessible through our website: www.youmakethedifference.net/books

To help this global shift at the local level all people need to ask is:

Q

What is the Unity in our Comm-unity? How can our highest aspirations for humanity and our planet be reflected in what we do locally, what we create together, and how we relate to each other?

> All that is required for any individual to become part of this natural, crucial and inevitable evolution is to make the choice to become part of the solution rather than be part of the problems in society.

When people are willing to offer some of their time, skill and experience to improve those things that affect their lives and the lives of those around them they could be making a significant positive difference to their society. To do this through participating in groups and becoming involved in projects is simple, empowering, mutually supportive, and, it can be a lot of fun!

MORE YOU MAKE THE DIFFERENCE BOOKS

Ripples created by our actions inevitably make some difference in the world. These books are intended to encourage and help people who want to make a positive difference to their lives and to the world around them.

**YOU MAKE THE DIFFERENCE
through
ENJOYABLE & EFFECTIVE MEETINGS**

Following the guidelines for constructive participation, for efficient chairing and supportive facilitation, adopting the suggested attitudes, implementing the methods, skills, tools, essential procedures and useful processes will guarantee improved effectiveness and enjoyment of any meeting.

**YOU MAKE THE DIFFERENCE
Through
EFFORTLESS FACILITATION**

This book is packed with suggestions for planning and designing meetings and events, useful methods and tips for facilitation, empowering and productive processes and a variety of ready-made meeting designs to fit many situations. The implementation of these will guarantee inexperienced facilitators becoming skillful and experienced facilitators becoming even more accomplished – effortlessly!

YOU MAKE THE DIFFERENCE
Through
ENJOYABLE & VALUABLE
VOLUNTEERING

This book contains simple and exciting methods for people to explore what skills and experience they could volunteer, where and how they can easily make their valuable contribution, how to look after themselves while effectively helping others and the many enjoyable ways in which volunteering will enrich their own lives.

YOU MAKE THE DIFFERENCE
Through
EMPOWERING VOLUNTEER MANAGMENT

This book contains many suggestions for finding, recruiting, supporting, empowering, managing and keeping volunteers. Following these guidelines and using the insights into what volunteers need to be efficient, effective, valuable and fulfilled in their roles, will guarantee empowered volunteers.

**YOU MAKE THE DIFFERENCE
Through
INSPIRING COMMUNITY
SUSTAINABILITY**

The answer to many of the difficulties facing society is creating a greater sense of community. This book is filled with information and insights, developed through decades of research and experience, on the elements essential for achieving sustainability in any form of community. Utilizing this information, adopting the suggested attitudes, and implementing the recommended systems and processes will guarantee greater sustainability in communities, whether they are rural or urban, traditional or intentional, Transition Towns or Ecovillages.

YOU MAKE THE DIFFERENCE
Through
SMART TALKING

Each time we open our mouths to speak we will inevitably have an impact upon those to whom we are talking. This book aims to show the consequences of having a negative impact and offers insightful suggestions for creating a positive effect. Following these guidelines and the suggested attitudes, skills and tools that can relieve stress, enhance relationships and improve communication in so many areas of life will guarantee anyone becoming a Smart Talker.

YOU MAKE THE DIFFERENCE
Through
SMART LISTENING

Each of us will inevitably have an impact upon the individuals to whom we listen that is either positive and beneficial or negative and potentially damaging to individuals and society. Implementing the attitudes, listening skills, tools and techniques suggested in this book will guarantee a positive effect that will greatly improve personal and working relationships, reduce conflict, enhance many areas of life and be supportive to people's confidence and self-esteem.

YOU MAKE THE DIFFERENCE
Through
SMART TALKING
& LISTENING TO CHILDREN

From the moment children are born they are learning to become the adults who will manage the future. What kind of future might adults be influencing through the way they talk and listen to children? This book is crammed with skills, tools, insights and suggestions on how adults can be supportive through their communication to the development of youngsters and contribute towards a safe, sustainable future in the hands of well adjusted, capable, empowered, responsible and caring people.

ABOUT
YOU MAKE THE DIFFERENCE

Tim and Kay Kay, the two generations of cultural creatives who founded YOU MAKE THE DIFFERENCE, believe that it is now essential for people to behave supportively with another, to become more engaged in their local community and to cooperate and work together for a sustainable future. The books and website are intended to encourage and support people to achieve the positive difference they wish to make in their lives and in the world around them.

To help with this, Kay Kay, the author, offers decades of experience gained in a variety of professions and cultures, and shares her practical philosophy, knowledge, skills and insights into beneficial ways of behaving, working and communicating with one another and contributing to society.

Tim, as collaborator, book designer, publisher and Webmaster, brings his creativity as an artist and writer, his in-depth knowledge of Buddhist philosophy and the skills and considerable experience gained through living, working and studying in many countries.

All the YOU MAKE THE DIFFERENCE books are intended to be enjoyable to read and easy to use - by everyone. The wealth of information is concisely written to be of benefit to professionals wishing to upgrade their skills; busy people working to make a difference in their communities and at the grassroots of their societies, and people from different cultures, especially those from the developing world, for whom English may be a 2nd or even 3rd language.

On the website: www.youmakethedifference.net there is more background information; GUIDES on a variety of interesting and useful subjects that are FREE to download and the opportunity for people to become part of the Global YOU MAKE THE DIFFERENCE network.

"We each make a difference in the world every moment through our words, actions and behavior, whether we are aware of it or not. The trick to being a smart human being is to choose to make a positive difference."

Kay Kay

Made in the USA
Charleston, SC
22 May 2013